CRYPTOGRAPHY, STEGANOGRAPHY AND DATA SECURITY

THE TARGET STORE DATA BREACHES

EXAMINATION AND INSIGHT

CRYPTOGRAPHY, STEGANOGRAPHY AND DATA SECURITY

Additional books in this series can be found on Nova's website under the Series tab.

Additional e-books in this series can be found on Nova's website under the e-book tab.

CRYPTOGRAPHY, STEGANOGRAPHY AND DATA SECURITY

THE TARGET STORE DATA BREACHES

EXAMINATION AND INSIGHT

MARIANNA HARDY
EDITOR

New York

For permission to use material from this book please contact us:
Telephone 631-231-7269; Fax 631-231-8175
Web Site: http://www.novapublishers.com

Library of Congress Cataloging-in-Publication Data

ISBN: 978-1-63321-269-5

Published by Nova Science Publishers, Inc. † New York

CONTENTS

PREFACE

In November and December of 2013, cyber-criminals breached the data security of Target, one of the largest U.S. retail chains, stealing the personal and financial information of millions of customers. On December 19, 2013, Target confirmed that some 40 million credit and debit card account numbers had been stolen. On January 10, 2014, Target announced that personal information, including the names, addresses, phone numbers, and email addresses of up to 70 million customers, was also stolen during the data breach. A report by the Senate Committee on Commerce in March 2014 concluded that Target missed opportunities to prevent the data breach. This book answers some frequently asked questions about the Target breach, including what is known to have happened in the breach, and what costs may result. It also examines some of the broader issues common to data breaches, including how the payment system works, how cybersecurity costs are shared and allocated within the payment system, who bears the losses in such breaches more generally, what emerging cybersecurity technologies may help prevent them, and what role the government could play in encouraging their adoption. The book addresses policy issues discussed in congressional hearings and describes some of the legislation that Congress has introduced to deal with these issues. This book also presents an explanation of how the Target breach occurred, based on media reports and expert analyses that have been published since Target publicly acknowledged this breach.

Chapter 1 – In November and December of 2013, cyber-criminals breached the data security of Target, one of the largest U.S. retail chains, stealing the personal and financial information of millions of customers. On December 19, 2013, Target confirmed that some 40 million credit and debit card account numbers had been stolen. On January 10, 2014, Target announced that personal information, including the names, addresses, phone numbers, and email addresses of up to 70 million customers, was also stolen during the data breach. A report by the Senate Committee on Commerce in March 2014 concluded that Target missed opportunities to prevent the data breach.

To date, Target has reported data breach costs of $61 million. Independent sources have made back-of-the-envelope estimates ranging from $240 million to $2.2 billion, in fraudulent charges alone. This does not include additional potential costs to consumers concerned about their personal information or credit histories, potential fines or penalties to Target, financial institutions or others, or any costs to Target related to a loss of consumer confidence. The breach was among the largest in U.S. history.

Chapter 2 – In November and December 2013, cyber thieves executed a successful cyber attack against Target, one of the largest retail companies in the United States. The attackers surreptitiously gained access to Target's computer network, stole the financial and personal information of as many as 110 million Target customers, and then removed this sensitive information from Target's network to a server in Eastern Europe. This report presents an explanation of how the Target breach occurred, based on media reports and expert analyses that have been published since Target publicly acknowledged this breach on December 19, 2013. Although the complete story of how this breach took place may not be known until Target completes its forensic examination of the breach, facts already available in the public record provide a great deal of useful information about the attackers' methods and Target's defenses.

This report analyzes what has been reported to date about the Target data breach, using the "intrusion kill chain" framework, an analytical tool introduced by Lockheed Martin security researchers in 2011, and today widely used by information security professionals in both the public and the private sectors. This analysis suggests that Target missed a number of opportunities along the kill chain to stop the attackers and prevent the massive data breach.

Chapter 3 – This is the Statement of Senator Patrick Leahy, Chairman, Senate Judiciary Committee.

Chapter 4 – This is the Statement of Delara Derakhshani, Policy Counsel, Consumers Union.

Chapter 5 – This is the Testimony of John Mulligan, Executive Vice President and CFO, Target Corporation.

Chapter 6 – This is the Testimony of Michael R. Kingston, Senior Vice President and CIO, The Neiman Marcus Group.

Chapter 7 – This is the Testimony of Fran Rosch, Senior Vice President, Security Products and Services, Endpoint and Mobility, Symantec Corporation.

Chapter 8 – This is the Statement of Edith Ramirez, Chairwoman, Federal Trade Commission.

Chapter 9 – This is the Testimony of William Noonan, Deputy Special Agent in Charge, Criminal Investigative Division, U.S. Secret Service.

Chapter 10 – This is the Statement of Mythili Raman, Acting Assistant Attorney General, Criminal Division, United States Department of Justice.

Chapter 11 – This is the Written Questions for the Record of Chairman Leahy for John J. Mulligan, Executive Vice President and Chief Financial Officer, Target Corporation, to Senator Patrick Leahy, Chairman of the Senate Judiciary Committee, dated February 11, 2014.

In: The Target Store Data Breaches
Editor: Marianna Hardy

ISBN: 978-1-63321-269-5

Chapter 1

THE TARGET DATA BREACH: FREQUENTLY ASKED QUESTIONS*

N. Eric Weiss and Rena S. Miller

SUMMARY

In November and December of 2013, cyber-criminals breached the data security of Target, one of the largest U.S. retail chains, stealing the personal and financial information of millions of customers. On December 19, 2013, Target confirmed that some 40 million credit and debit card account numbers had been stolen. On January 10, 2014, Target announced that personal information, including the names, addresses, phone numbers, and email addresses of up to 70 million customers, was also stolen during the data breach. A report by the Senate Committee on Commerce in March 2014 concluded that Target missed opportunities to prevent the data breach.

To date, Target has reported data breach costs of $61 million. Independent sources have made back-of-the-envelope estimates ranging from $240 million to $2.2 billion, in fraudulent charges alone. This does not include additional potential costs to consumers concerned about their personal information or credit histories, potential fines or penalties to Target, financial institutions or

* This is an edited, reformatted and augmented version of a Congressional Research Service publication R43496, prepared for Members and Committees of Congress dated March April 22, 2014.

others, or any costs to Target related to a loss of consumer confidence. The breach was among the largest in U.S. history.

Consumer concern over the scale of this data breach has fueled further congressional attention on the Target breach and on data security and data breaches more broadly. In the wake of Target's revelations, Congress has held seven hearings by six different committees related to these topics between February 3 and April 2, 2014. In addition to examining the events surrounding the Target breach, hearings have focused on preventing such data breaches, improving data security standards, better protecting consumers' personal data, and providing notice to consumers when their data have been compromised.

Policy options discussed in these hearings include federal legislation to require notification to consumers when their data have been breached; legislation to potentially increase Federal Trade Commission (FTC) powers and authorities over companies' data security; and legislation that could create a federal standard for the general quality or reasonableness of companies' data security. The broader question of whether the government should play a role in encouraging or even requiring companies to adopt newer data security technologies was also broached.

Legislation in the 113th Congress that addresses these various issues in different ways includes S. 1897, S. 1927, S. 1976, S. 1995, S. 1193, H.R. 1468, and H.R. 3990. In 2014, the Obama Administration has encouraged Congress to pass legislation on data security and data breach notification. Attorney General Eric Holder issued a public statement in the wake of the Target breach on February 24, 2014, urging Congress to pass a federal data breach notification law which would hold entities accountable when they fail to keep sensitive information safe. The FTC also called on Congress to pass a federal data security law, including data breach notification, and to increase the commission's explicit statutory authority over data security issues.

This report answers some frequently asked questions about the Target breach, including what is known to have happened in the breach, and what costs may result. It also examines some of the broader issues common to data breaches, including how the payment system works, how cybersecurity costs are shared and allocated within the payment system, who bears the losses in such breaches more generally, what emerging cybersecurity technologies may help prevent them, and what role the government could play in encouraging their adoption. The report addresses policy issues discussed in congressional hearings and describes some of the legislation that Congress has introduced to deal with these issues.

WHAT IS KNOWN ABOUT THE TARGET BREACH?

According to Target,[1] in November and December of 2013, information on 40 million payment cards (credit, debit, and ATM cards) and personally identifiable information (PII) on 70 million customers was compromised. The Secret Service has announced that it is investigating the data breach, but has released no details.[2] In congressional hearings, Target's executive vice president testified that an intruder used a vendor's access to Target's system to place malware on point-of-sale (POS) registers. The malware captured credit and debit card information before it was encrypted, which would render it more difficult (or impossible) to read. In addition, the intruder captured some strongly encrypted personal identification numbers (PIN).

It is very unlikely that all 40 million payment cards compromised at Target will be used in fraudulent transactions. Some cards will be canceled before they are used, some attempts to use valid cards will be denied by the issuing financial institutions, and there will be no attempt to make fraudulent use of some.

According to media reports, some financial institutions have issued new cards to all of their cardholders, and others have decided to depend on antifraud monitoring. Initially, Wells Fargo, Citibank, and JPMorgan Chase replaced debit cards, but not credit cards, while Bank of America and U.S. Bank are depending on fraud detection.[3]

Cost Estimates

Target has reported that in its fourth quarter of its 2013 fiscal year, which ended February 1, 2014, it had $61 million in pretax expenses due to the data breach, and expected to recover $44 million from insurance, resulting in a net cost of $17 million before tax, or $11 million after tax.[4] This $11 million is $1.53 per card before insurance and tax deductions or $0.28 per card after insurance and taxes. The $61 million included the cost of investigating the breach, providing credit-monitoring services, increasing call center staffing, other professional services, and "an accrual related to the expected payment card networks' counterfeit fraud losses and non-ordinary course operating expenses."[5] Target stated that more than 80 lawsuits have been filed against it, but that it is confident that it will prevail in court.

Jefferies, an investment bank, quotes an industry expert, Julie Conroy, who estimates that 4.8-7.2 million cards will be used to charge $1.4-$2.2 billion fraudulently.[6] Ms. Conroy said that card issuers are liable for the fraud except when the card is not present at the time of the purchase (e.g., telephone and online purchases).[7] Ms. Conroy is quoted by Jefferies as estimating that the Payment Cards Industry (PCI) Council, founded in 2006 by the main payment card companies (Visa, Master Card, American Express, Discover, and JCB) to establish industry security standards, could fine Target between $400 million and $1.1 billion.

According to Jefferies, Ms. Conroy said that, in general, the largest payment card issuers are better at fraud detection than the other issuers. She estimated that 10%-15% of the cards issued by the financial institutions with the most sophisticated detection systems would have fraudulent charges, while 20%-30% of the cards issued by other financial institutions would have fraudulent charges.

Others suggest that this could overestimate the volume of fraudulent transactions that will occur in the Target case. For example, Ellen Richey, chief enterprise risk officer of Visa, testified that 2%-5% of compromised Visa cards experience fraud.[8] Using the same $300 of fraud per card that Ms. Conroy used, fraudulent charges could be $240-$600 million.

To provide some context, Target has reported 2013 net income of $3.0 billion and stockholders' equity of $16.6 billion.[9] If Target's cost of the data breach were to be a $1.1 billion PCI fine, that would be 37% of their 2013 net income or 7% of 2013 stockholder's equity. On the other hand, combining Ms. Conroy's assumption that PCI fines could be 30%-50% of fraudulent charges with Visa's low-end estimate of 2% of cards being used fraudulently, the estimated PCI fine would be $72 million, which is 2% of 2013 net income and less than 1% of 2013 stockholders' equity.

Timeline of Known Events

According to testimony of John J. Mulligan, executive vice president and chief financial officer of Target, the key dates in the Target breach are as follows:

- November 12, 2013, intruders breached Target's computer system. The intrusion was detected by Target's security systems, but the company's security professionals took no action until notified by law enforcement of the breach.

- December 12, 2013, the Department of Justice (DOJ) notified Target that there was suspicious activity involving payment cards that had been used at Target.
- December 13, 2013, Target met with DOJ and the U.S. Secret Service.
- December 14, 2013, Target hired outside experts to conduct a thorough forensic investigation.
- December 15, 2013, Target confirmed that malware had been installed and that most of the malware had been removed.
- December 16 and 17, 2013, Target notified payment processors and card networks that a breach had occurred.
- December 18, 2013, Target removed the remaining malware.
- December 19, 2013, Target made a public announcement of the breach.
- December 27, 2013, Target announced the theft of the encrypted PIN data.
- January 9, 2014, Target discovered the theft of PII.
- January 10, 2014, Target announced the PII theft.

Target estimates that the 40 million payment card and 70 million PII data breaches have at least 12 million people in common, making 98 million the maximum number of customers affected.[10]

Fazio Mechanical Services, which provided heating, ventilation, and air conditioning (HVAC) services for Target, has said it was used to breach Target's payment system.[11] A Fazio computer authorized to submit contract billing and project management information to Target reportedly was compromised by intruders. According to some media reports, Fazio was the victim of a phishing email containing malware that was used to install other malware in Target's network, including its POS system[12] that records payment card transactions.[13]

Payment card companies require any business accepting payment cards to follow PCI rules regarding security of their payment card processing. Target has testified that its systems were reviewed in September 2013 and certified as compliant.

The magnetic stripes on the back of U.S. credit cards are not encrypted. According to media reports, malware known as a "memory scraper" captured information from a customer's payment card by reading the POS system's memory before it was encrypted.[14]

After the initial announcement of the Target data breach, other possibly related data breaches were reported, including at Neiman Marcus (a luxury retailer), Michaels (an arts and crafts retailer), and White Lodging (a hotel management company) who had been notified by law enforcement that they had suffered related data breaches.[15]

In summary,[16]

- It appears that someone obtained a vendor's credentials to access the Target vendor billing and invoicing system.
- It appears that access to the vendor billing and invoicing system was escalated to access into Target's POS system.
- It appears that this was used to introduce malware into the system.
- It appears that warnings about this malware were initially ignored.
- It appears that Target software was used to spread the malware to virtually all of Target's POS devices.
- It appears that the credit card data were stored in innocuously named files and sent to servers outside Target's system and then on to other servers.
- It appears that warnings about transmitting the data were ignored.[17]

How Does the Payment Card System Work?

The two basic approaches to payment card systems differ in the number of parties to the transaction. The most common is the four-party system, which is used by MasterCard and Visa. This system involves a *merchant*, an *acquirer* (the merchant's bank), the *issuer* (the customer's bank), and the *cardholder*.[18] The alternative called the three-party system—used by companies such as Diners Club, Discover, and American Express—consists of the merchant, the payment card company, and the cardholder.

Four-Party Transactions

Figure 1 illustrates a typical purchase using the four-party system.

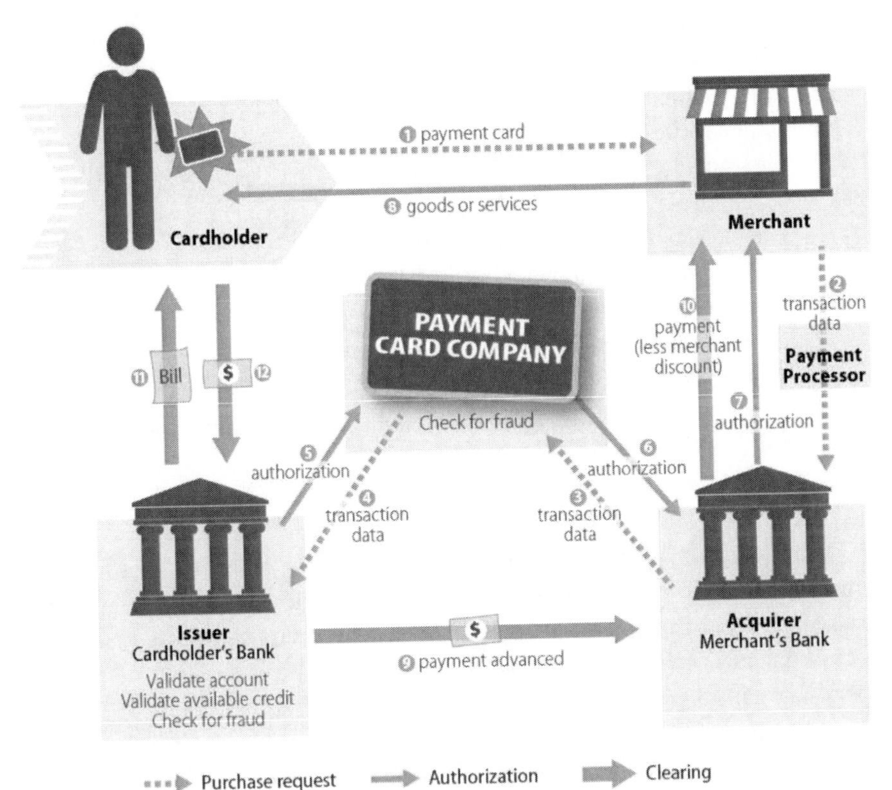

Source: CRS based on MasterCard 2013 Annual Report and Visa 2013 Annual Report.

Note: The "Payment Card" is also called the "network provider," especially in the case of ATM and debit card transactions.

Figure 1. Four-Party Payment Card Transaction.

1. A *cardholder* presents a payment card to a retailer to pay for merchandise. The card is "swiped" and information about the card and the purchases is sent to the retailer's computers in a secured room.
2. This transaction is transmitted to the *acquirer* (i.e., the retailer's bank).
3. The acquirer relays the transaction information to the *payment card company*, which may conduct an anti-fraud analysis.
4. The payment card sends this information to the *issuer*, the bank that issued the payment card. The issuer verifies that the account is valid, that the cardholder has available credit, and it may perform additional anti-fraud analysis.

5. The issuer notifies the payment card company of its decision to authorize (or not to authorize) the transaction.
6. The payment card company notifies the acquirer of the issuer's authorization decision.
7. The acquirer notifies the merchant of the issuer's authorization decision.
8. The cardholder leaves with their purchases.
9. The issuing financial institution (bank, credit union, etc.) pays the acquirer and posts the amount of the purchase to the cardholder's account. The acquirer receives the amount minus an interchange fee charged by the payment network.
10. The acquirer deducts a fee[19] and credits the merchant with the balance.
11. The cardholder receives a monthly bill.
12. The cardholder makes a payment on the monthly bill.

Both the interchange fees and the merchant discounts depend on a number of factors related to risk and cost. Was the card physically present or was the transaction done by telephone or Internet? Was the receipt signed or was a PIN used? What business is the merchant in? What has been the card network's experience with the merchant? Is the customer in a foreign country? Do the funds have to be converted to another currency? Is the card a credit card, a debit card, or a prepaid card? Is the card a standard, premium, or affluent card? Is the cardholder an individual or a business?

Three-Party Transactions

In the three-party system, the merchant sends the transaction information directly to the payment cards, which sends the funds to the merchant (less fees) and lends the cardholder the funds for the purchase.

In 2013, four-party payment cards (Visa and MasterCard) dominated the payments system. In 2013, as measured in dollars, Visa's share was 56% and MasterCard's was 26%.[20] American Express's share in 2013 was 15% and Discover's was 3%.

Many merchants contract with outside payment processors to manage the payment process between the POS and the acquirer (four-party system) or the payment card (three-party system). The payment processors are approved by PCI. Payment processors include large international banks, such as JPMorgan Chase; financial services companies, such as Heartland Payments and First

Data; technology startups, such as SquaredUp; and established technology firms, such as Google and Yahoo.

In theory, credit card security can be compromised anywhere in the system: at the point of sale, transmission of the information, at either of the banks, or at the payment card company. An attacker can come directly from the outside, or it can infiltrate an authorized user to obtain access.

WHY DO CYBERSECURITY BREACHES, ESPECIALLY IN THE RETAIL INDUSTRY, KEEP HAPPENING?

There are economic, technological, and strategic reasons why payment card breaches continue to occur. The crime can be profitable and those involved are thought to have relatively little risk of arrest. Merchants, banks, and payment cards share costs and benefits, but minimizing the cost of a new technology to deter payment card breaches may involve shifting the expense to someone else. Cyber technology and business efficiencies for merchants, banks, payment cards, payment processors, and cybercriminals are constantly evolving.

Obtaining cardholder information has been profitable, and obtaining the information on thousands or millions of cardholders has been even more profitable. Although law enforcement authorities try to arrest and prosecute those responsible, international cooperation can be less than what might be desired, which reduces the risks to those responsible for the breaches.

The incentives to improve cybersecurity are divided along the transaction path of merchant, acquirer (the merchant's bank), payment cards, issuing bank, and cardholder. In the aftermath of the Target case, some merchants have complained that the current magnetic stripe and signature system should be replaced with a Chip and PIN system, which would use the EMV computer chip—named after EuroPay, MasterCard and Visa, which developed it—to encrypt payment information.[21] The payment card industry has announced that effective October 1, 2015, liability for fraudulent transactions (except for ATMs and gas stations) will be assigned to the merchant or issuer that is not Chip and Signature compliant.

For a number of years, payment card companies have argued that Chip and Signature was unnecessary in the United States because POS terminals[22] are connected to the payment system allowing for immediate (real-time) approval. One advantage of Chip and Signature/PIN is that it can be used to approve purchases even if no computer connection is available to the issuing bank and payment card company.[23]

Another advantage is that Chip-based systems are supposed to make it more difficult for unauthorized persons to duplicate payment cards compared with the cards used in the United States presently.

Some banks in the United States have begun issuing Chip and Signature cards to certain customers.[24] According to a multi-industry trade group, the Smart Card Alliance, Chip and Signature cards are currently issued by 17 financial institutions, including some of the largest volume issuers.[25] Outside of the United States, more than 75% of terminals and 45% of payment cards use an EMV chip.[26]

In short, chip-based cards could reduce fraud because they are more difficult (but not impossible) to forge. On the other hand, fraud involving Internet, telephone, and mail orders does not require a payment card to be present. Compared with signature-based authentication, PINs make it harder (but not impossible) to use a stolen card.

HOW BIG ARE CREDIT CARD DATA BREACH LOSSES?

Many types of costs affect merchants, banks, payment cards, payment processors, consumers, and the party whose information is compromised. The response of those affected has an impact on the cost per record and the total cost. In 2007, Forrester Research surveyed 28 companies and estimated data breach costs of $90 to $305 per record.[27] If this estimate is accurate for the Target case, the cost to Target's 40 million cards compromised could result in costs of $3.6 billion to $12.2 billion.

According to research by the Ponemon Institute,[28] factors influencing the losses in data breaches include industry, existence of a privacy and data protection security policy, the type of information handled, the most likely cause of a data breach, whether data are stored on laptops or removable devices, whether data are encrypted, whether there is a full-time information security manager, number of employees, where in the world the company operates, policies concerning remote access to sensitive data, user authentication technology, headquarters location, and the number of sensitive records.

Ponemon estimated that a 2013 data breach in the retail sector would cost an average of $122 per record as compared with an average of $254 per card in the financial sector, and $304 in the health care sector.[29] Costs included hiring outside experts, hiring a call center, the cost of cardholder credit monitoring, providing discounts to cardholders, reduced sales, and the cost of the staff response. If Target's cost turns out to be $122 per record, the total cost of the Target breach would be $4.9 billion.

This section continues by looking at who bears the various costs of the payment breach in the first instance. It looks at the costs unique to merchants, banks, the payment processor, and consumers. It also examines the costs to the party breached. Ultimately private contracts among the various parties in the payment system and lawsuits can reallocate these costs.

The cost of reversing fraudulent transactions follows the entire chain of processing a payment card transaction, but—assuming that the funds can be recovered—this cost is likely to be relatively small.

Costs Unique to Merchants

In the case of payment card fraud, the issuing bank may issue a *chargeback* and retrieve the funds paid to the merchant who is unlikely to be able to retrieve the merchandise. Chargebacks can affect both the merchant breached and other merchants.

Sales may decline if customers lose confidence in the merchant and shop less frequently or purchase less when they shop. Target reports that its fourth quarter 2014 U.S. sales decreased 2.5% and were "meaningfully softer following the announcement."[30] Among retailers not reporting recent data breaches, Walmart's comparable sales declined 0.4% in their fourth quarter 2014,[31] and Costco's comparable U.S. sales increased 4% in the 18 weeks ending January 5, 2014.[32]

Academic research in general finds that payment breaches have little long-lasting impact on a company's *stock price*, and this appears to be true for Target. Between December 18, 2013 (the day before the breach's public announcement), and March 3, 2014 (the first trading day in March 2014), Target's stock declined 0.3%, but Costco's stock declined 2.3% and Walmart's stock declined 4.9%.

Costs Unique to Card Issuers

One cost to issuers is the cost of issuing *replacement cards*. In the recent Target case, a figure of $10 per card issued has been widely used.[33] This estimate appears to include the cost of obtaining new blank cards, embossing the cards, modifying accounts with the new account numbers, notifying cardholders, delivering the cards, and using a call center to answer questions related to the cancellation of the old cards and the issuance of the new ones.

Card issuers face the decision of which cards should be replaced. There may be a difference between the cards potentially compromised and those actually compromised. Not all cards actually compromised will be used in fraudulent transactions. Issuers that are better at detecting and preventing fraudulent charges may choose to replace fewer cards than other issuers.

Costs Unique to Payment Processors

Some merchants decide to contract out payment processing to third-party contractors that connect a merchant with the acquiring financial institution. Services offered by payment processors range from handling the entire credit card process from POS to payment to the merchant's account and accounting to assessments of a merchant's compliance with PCI standards. Small merchants use payment processors because they do not have the need for a full-time staff of computer security specialists, and large merchants use them as a form of outsourcing for greater efficiency or to concentrate on the basic business.

Payment processors can be the victims of payment card data breaches. For example, in March 2012, Global Payments, a merchant payment processor, reported a data breach. "Certain" card networks temporarily suspended Global Payments as an authorized provider.[34] Global Payments reported that as of May 31, 2013, its costs (before insurance payments) were $156.9 million consisting of $121.2 million for professional fees for investigation and remediation, incentive fees to business partners, credit monitoring, and identity protection, and an additional $35.7 million in fraud losses, fines and charges imposed by the card networks. Insurance covered $20.0 million. A class action lawsuit filed against Global Payments was dismissed.

According to media reports,[35] about 1.5 million payment cards were affected, making the cost per card $104.

Costs Unique to Payment Cards

The four-party payment card companies (e.g., MasterCard and Visa) appear to largely avoid financial responsibility for data breaches and payment card fraud. In three-party payment systems, card companies (e.g., Diners Club, Discover, and American Express) bear credit risk from lending a cardholder the funds to pay the merchant. In the four-party system, it is the issuing bank, not the payment card company, that bears the credit risk. Thus, the issuing bank, not the payment card company, in a four-party payment system, has potential exposure to the costs of payment card fraud. In the three-party network, the payment card company re-issues compromised cards, but in the four-party system it is the issuer's responsibility.

An examination of MasterCard's and Visa's annual reports found no explicit mention of expenses incurred because of fraud and data breaches. In contrast, American Express, Global Payments, and Heartland all mentioned these expenses.

Costs Unique to Consumers

Many costs to consumers can be difficult to value, but some are precisely known. Legally, the maximum cost to a consumer of a stolen credit card is $50.[36] The cost to a consumer of a stolen debit card varies depending on how quickly the consumer notifies the card issuer: $50 if the issuer is notified within two business days discovering the loss or $500 if the notification is made more than two days after discovery and less than 60 days after receiving a statement. In practice, the payment card issuers do not charge a cardholder for fraudulent transactions. The breached organization frequently provides free credit monitoring; consumers are to identify the fraudulent transactions and notify the card issuer. Consumers may also be subject to increased identity theft risks. Additional consumer costs include the loss of privacy, the time to monitor card use more closely, and the inconvenience of getting new cards.

Costs Incurred by the Party Breached

The cost to the entity breached can include lost sales, a damaged reputation, forensic examination, hiring outside experts, notifying cardholders, creating or expanding call centers to answer cardholders questions, offering cardholders credit or identity monitoring, additional compensation to customers, hiring an external public relations firm for damage control, legal expenses, increased regulatory oversight, fines by regulators or industry groups, diversion of staff to dealing with the breach, and enhanced security.

Table 1. Summary of Loss Estimates from Selected Credit Card Data Breaches

Source	Loss Estimates		Comments
	Total per Incident	Per Card	
Ponemon (2013)	$4.9 billion	$122	General retail estimate
Jefferies (2014)	$1.4-$2.2 billion fraud $400 million-$1.1 billion PCI fines	$35-$55 fraud $10-$28 PCI fines	Target, limited costs considered 40 million cards
Visa/Jefferies (2014)	$240-$600 million	$6-$10	Replace fraud rates used by Jefferies with Visa's fraud rates 40 million cards
Target (2013)	$61 million gross $17 million after insurance $11 million after insurance and taxes	$1.10 $0.28	Reported for fourth quarter 2013 only 40 million cards Total costs not yet known
Global Payments (2012)	$156.9 million	$104	Global Payments 1.5 million cards

Sources: Ponemon Institute, "2013 Cost of Data Breach Study: United States," p. 6, at http://www.symantec.com/content/en/us/about/media/pdfs/b-cost-of-a-data-breach-us-report-2013.en-us.pdf? om_ext_cid=biz_socmed_twitter_facebook_marketwire_linkedin_2013Jun_worldwide_CostofaDataBreach; Daniel Binder, "Jefferies Equity Research, Americas: Target," January 29, 2014; Testimony of Ellen Richey, Chief Enterprise Risk Officer, Visa, Inc. before U.S. Congress, Senate Committee on Commerce, Science, and Transportation, *Hearing on Protecting Personal Consumer Information from Cyber Attacks and Data Breaches*, 113th Cong., 2nd sess., March 26, 2014, p. 12, at http://www.commerce.senate.gov/public/?a=Files.Serve&File_id=9d2d04c0-0aa2-4a07-9a11-81d74a7339a8; Target Corporation, "Form 10-K," Fiscal Year Ended February 2, 2013, p.

17, at http://edgar.sec.gov/Archives/edgar/data/27419/000104746913003100/a2213506z10-k.htm#da18701_part_i; and Global Payments, "Form 10-K for the Fiscal Year Ended May 31, 2013," p. 62, at http://www.sec.gov/Archives/edgar/data/1123360/000112336013000025/gpn20130531-10k.htm.

WHO ULTIMATELY BEARS THE LOSSES?

In data breaches such as Target's, who is liable for the costs associated with such data breaches depends on a web of individual contracts among retailers, the banks that issue cards and handle payments, credit card companies such as Visa and MasterCard, payment processors authorized by the credit card companies to process payments at the point of sale, and even contracts between a retailer and its third-party service provider (such as Target's HVAC contractor).[37] These contracts allocate liability, the right to indemnification for breaches, and set certain duties and standards for cybersecurity protections, such as in the individually negotiated "representations and warranties" sections of such contracts.

Generally, the issuing financial institution pays the cost of card reissuance and for fraudulent charges made on compromised cards. Banks may sue the retailer for employing inadequate data security systems. In the case of Target, a number of smaller financial institutions have filed class action lawsuits against Target under Minnesota state law, which reportedly has strict standards on data breach notification and minimum cybersecurity standards.[38] (Target is headquartered in Minnesota.) The financial institutions claim damages, among other things, for costs associated with notifying customers of issues related to the Target data breach, closing out and opening new customer accounts, reissuing cards, and refunding customer losses resulting from unauthorized charges.[39]

In some past data breach cases, merchants accused of using lax systems have paid significant costs of their own. Following a 2007 data breach at T.J. Maxx involving about 45 million debit and credit cards, TJX, the owner of T.J. Maxx, paid out $65 million in settlement costs to Visa alone.[40] In sum, courts have been called upon to play key roles in deciding who should bear losses from data breaches like Target's. This is often done on a case-by-case basis, and often litigated under a variety of state laws. This has led to a lack of uniformity in the outcomes.

This situation has led to calls from some academics and media observers for Congress to examine the issue of who ultimately is responsible for the losses and who is in the best position to prevent losses. Some have also called on Congress to craft policy solutions allocating liability to those best able to minimize the threat of cybercrime and thereby protect consumers at the least cost.[41] Because of the shared responsibility for cybersecurity over consumers' data, however, it may not be easy to determine which parties are in fact in the best position to minimize the threat of cybercrime and protect consumers.[42] This is because customers' data are necessarily shared by retailers, payment card companies, payment processors, and financial institutions. Because breaches may occur at any point along this chain, deciding who should bear the cost of cybersecurity may not be straightforward.

To date, congressional hearings on the Target breaches have tended to focus more on policy solutions, such as notifying consumers that data breaches have occurred, and increasing or clarifying the FTC's authority to sanction lax data security practices. They have not focused on whether or how to allocate shared responsibility to the parties best positioned to protect against cyber breaches.

WHAT INDUSTRY BEST PRACTICES HAVE BEEN ADOPTED?

The current payment card system in the United States is based on payment cards that have magnetic stripes on the back that contain the account number, cardholder name, service code, expiration date and other information in an unencrypted format.[43] This unencrypted information is necessarily read into the merchant's payment processing system unencrypted and potentially vulnerable for a fraction of a second. A secure card reader encrypts the data before sending it to the merchant's server for transmission to the acquiring bank, but it is theoretically possible to intercept the information inside the card reader before it has been encrypted.

Current PCI standards require encryption only when cardholder data are transmitted over public networks such as the Internet and when they are stored.[44] The magnetic stripe and signature card suffers from a number of weaknesses:

- Card information on the magnetic stripe is not encrypted and can easily be read.
- It reportedly is easy to forge magnetic stripe cards.[45]

- The signature on the back of a card provides a criminal with an example of the authentic signature, electronic signature pads can be difficult to sign in a manner that resembles the signature on the card, and the payment cards do not allow merchants to decline a transaction based on the signature of additional identity information, such as a driver's license.[46]

A strength of the magnetic stripe and signature system used in the United States is that authorization is largely done online and in real time. If a card is known to be stolen or forged, purchases will not be authorized.

Although the magnetic stripe and signature system is the standard in the United States, in most of the rest of the world, a system thought to be more secure, the Chip and PIN system, has been adopted. Arguably, the system used in the United States is not the best practice, but for some the cost of converting has outweighed the expected cost of the fraud.[47]

The Chip (also known as an EMV card after Europay, MasterCard, and Visa, which developed the standard) transmits the card information using encryption. The Chip, actually a small computer, can change the encryption every time it is used, making it nearly impossible for a criminal to capture and use cardholder information as it is transmitted and processed through the system.

Many Chip and PIN (or Chip and Signature) cards provide compatibility with magnetic stripe systems by adding a magnetic stripe, which potentially weakens their security. Chip and PIN is not foolproof; British researchers have demonstrated that there are a number of ways to bypass the security features of Chip and PIN cards.[48] One response to Chip-based security has been to use cards stolen or forged in countries that do not use Chip.

According to congressional testimony,[49] Chip and Signature increases security in two ways: (1) the information is encrypted and (2) it is more difficult to duplicate the Chip card. PIN adds another security factor that is called two-factor authentication.

The payment card companies have announced that effective October 1, 2015, a merchant or issuer who does not support Chip and Signature will be liable for most counterfeit card transactions.[50] For gas stations and ATMs the shift is scheduled to occur October 1, 2017.

According to Chris McWilton, MasterCard's president of North America, the argument in favor of using a signature instead of a PIN like that on debit and ATM cards is that a signature is easier than a PIN for customers.[51] He has also noted that banks will decide if it is worth their time to convert their systems to use a PIN and to issue PINs to customers.

According to Al Vrancart, a payment card consultant, the cost of producing a magnetic stripe card is about $0.50 compared with $2.20 to produce a chip card.[52] New POS terminals could cost $300-$600 each. Mallory Duncan, general counsel of the National Retail Federation, has testified that new POS terminals cost "an average of $1,000 or more per unit,"[53] but this estimate appears to include the cost of modifying the system and training employees.[54]

Emerging Technology Solutions

A number of technology solutions are emerging. *Tokenization* is a solution in which transaction information is stored on extremely secure servers known as vaults.[55] Each transaction is indexed by a token that is used to access it. This token is essentially a random number and designed so that outsiders cannot take a payment card or transaction and create the token. The token cannot be used as a credit card number, and it cannot be used by anyone but the merchant in the transaction. This places great reliance on the security of the vault and the tokenization process. It may make it more cumbersome for merchants to analyze customer records to send targeted messages about new products or sales.

With *encryption*, transaction information is transformed from plain text into an unintelligible format called cipher text.[56] Secret keys are required for encrypting and decrypting the information. Most Internet transactions use session encryption known as https (hypertext transfer protocol secure) instead of the unencrypted http (hypertext transfer protocol). The actual transaction information can be separately encrypted instead of or in addition to using https. Separate data encryption is used when storing the information in a database.

Mobile payments and *mobile banking*[57] are evolving alternatives in which mobile phones and tablets replace payment cards in financial transactions. The mobile device could be the customer's or the merchant could use a mobile device to process the customer's credit card. This raises questions about the security of the system: if a mobile device is stolen, can the owner's financial information be obtained and decrypted? If the customer is using an account with the merchant, how secure is the implementation? Is the transmission between the customer and the merchant secure? What are the security issues for various transmission technologies such as Bluetooth and near field communications (NFC), both of which allow the transaction to be completed without physical contact between the mobile device and the POS terminal? If the merchant is using a mobile device, what are its security strengths and weaknesses?

WHAT POLICY OPTIONS ARE BEING DISCUSSED?

This section discusses selected policy options that have been raised in congressional hearings held on data security and breaches following the Target breach.[58]

Passing a Federal Data Breach Notification Law

In each of the hearings related to the Target breach, various Members of Congress raised the possibility of a federal data breach notification law. Bills have been introduced in the 113th and earlier Congresses that would include some form of federal notification requirement for data security breaches. As will be discussed, 47 states presently have data breach notification laws.[59]

The phrase "data breach notification" is somewhat ambiguous, particularly when details such as personal information are introduced into the equation. Generally speaking, however, a data security breach occurs when there is unauthorized access to sensitive personally identifiable information (PII) that could compromise the confidentiality or integrity of data. "Data breach notification" involves mandating that the company holding the PII notify those whose PII was compromised.[60] Currently, only a few specific sectors of the private-sector economy are required by federal law to notify consumers when a data breach may have compromised their personal information, or PII.[61] These include certain financial institutions covered by the Gramm-Leach-BlileyAct62 and certain health care entities covered by the Health Insurance Portability and Accountability Act (HIPAA)[63] and the Health Information Technology for Economic and Clinical Health Act (HITECH Act).[64] There is no comprehensive federal law governing the protection of data held by private actors.[65] However, certain sectors are subject to cybersecurity obligations that may include data security.[66] Nor is there any comprehensive federal law requiring notification of breaches of such private data.

According to the National Conference of State Legislatures, currently 47 states, the District of Columbia, Puerto Rico, Guam, and the U.S. Virgin Islands have passed laws requiring notification of security breaches involving personal information.[67] Three states have not passed such laws: Alabama, New Mexico, and South Dakota.[68] California in 2002 became the first state to pass such a law.[69]

Businesses have complained about the patchwork of numerous, separate data breach notification laws[70] they are required to comply with, citing burdensomeness and inefficiency.[71] Business groups representing the financial and retail sectors, such as the Financial Services Roundtable and the National Retail Federation, have recently called for passage of a federal data breach notification law.[72] Some state regulators, state attorneys general, and certain consumer groups have voiced concerns that a federal law could preempt state laws and prevent states from mandating stricter notification standards.[73] A stronger federal data breach notification law, by contrast, appears to be more attractive to consumer groups.[74] A number of businesses have called for enactment of a federal notification law as it may result in cost savings, by potentially eliminating the need to comply with 47 individual state laws.[75] In addition, the executive branch has voiced support for a federal data breach notification law.[76] Recent media reports have suggested that bipartisan consensus may be building around the necessity of a federal data breach notification law, although details remain divergent between various bills and proposals.[77]

Generally, data breach notification laws include several components and address topics such as (1) which entities must comply with the law; (2) what information is being protected, and how a security breach or data breach is defined; (3) what degree of actual harm must occur, if any, for notice to be triggered; (4) how and when must notice be delivered; (5) are there any exceptions or safe harbors; (6) to what degree does this preempt state law and how does the law relate to other federal laws; and (7) what penalties, enforcement authorities, and remedies for those harmed does it create.[78]

The data breach notification bills introduced in the 113th Congress (S. 1897, S. 1193, S. 1927, S. 1976, S. 1995, H.R. 1468 and H.R. 3990)[79] address these elements in varying ways. Some of these bills contain express preemption clauses that could potentially displace certain state laws on data breach notification in order to create a uniform data breach notification standard.

Modifying Federal Trade Commission Statutory Powers

Some in Congress have called for passage of a law to strengthen the Federal Trade Commission's (FTC's) statutory authority to penalize businesses that fail to adequately protect consumers' personally identifiable information.[80] The FTC pursues enforcement actions against companies for failing to protect consumers' personal information.[81]

Currently, the FTC relies on its statutory powers under Section 5 of the Federal Trade Commission Act[82] to pursue data security violations. First, if a company makes materially misleading statements or omissions relating to an entity's data security practices and such statements or omissions are likely to mislead reasonable consumers, the FTC has argued that a company has engaged in unfair and deceptive practices prohibited by Section 5.[83] The company can agree with the FTC, negotiate a consent agreement with the FTC, or deny the FTC's claim. In this latter situation, the FTC could sue the company, alleging they engaged in unfair and deceptive practices prohibited under Section 5.[84] The FTC has reported that it has settled more than 30 matters on these grounds alone, in challenging companies' express or implied claims that they provided reasonable security for personal data.[85] Second, if a company's data security practices either "cause or are likely to cause substantial injury to consumers that is not reasonably avoidable by consumers nor are outweighed by benefits to consumers or to competition," the FTC has argued that those practices can be found to violate Section 5 of the Federal Trade Commission Act.[86] The FTC stated that it has settled more than 20 cases based on such allegations that a failure to reasonably safeguard consumer data was an unfair trade practice.[87]

Despite the FTC's total of 50 settlements broadly related to data security since 2001, the Federal Trade Commission Act does not contain explicit statutory power for the FTC to levy civil penalties specifically for unfair or deceptive trade practices related to data breaches.[88] The remedies agreed to in the settlements include the company agreeing to cease the unfair or deceptive trade practice but not paying extra penalties.[89] For example, the FTC reached a data security settlement with TRENDnet, which involved a video camera designed to allow consumers to monitor their homes remotely.[90] While TRENDnet marketed the cameras for in-home monitoring and claimed in product descriptions that the cameras were "secure," TRENDnet allegedly had software that left them open to online viewing by anyone with the cameras' web addresses, resulting in hackers posting 700 consumers' live feeds on the Internet.[91] Pursuant to a settlement with the FTC, TRENDnet must maintain a comprehensive security program, obtain outside audits, notify consumers about the security issues and about software updates to correct them, and provide affected customers with free technical support for two years.[92] But the FTC does not possess explicit statutory powers to impose monetary penalties or punitive fines on companies, such as TRENDnet or others, for unfair or deceptive trade practices related to a data breach.[93] The FTC has asked Congress to pass legislation making explicit its authority in this area.[94] The agency argues that having the explicit authority to impose fines or penalties as a result of an unfair or deceptive trade practice due to a data breach could provide a more useful deterrent effect.[95] The FTC has also requested that it be given express statutory authority to issue rules and regulations and jurisdiction over non-profit companies, which may also store consumers' personal data.[96]

The validity of the FTC's authority to pursue a company's data breach practices has recently been challenged in federal court.[97] Some had predicted that the outcome of the court case could have affected the FTC's current enforcement authority over data security.[98] In June 2012, following intermittent data breaches between 2008 and 2010, the FTC sued Wyndham hotel chains for allegedly misrepresenting the security measures the company took to protect consumers' personal information.[99] In response, Wyndham filed a motion to dismiss the lawsuit in 2013.[100] Wyndham claimed that "Section 5's prohibition on 'unfair' trade practices does not give the FTC authority to prescribe data-security standards for the private sector, particularly through selective enforcement actions that seek to impose after-the-fact Section 5 liability without any fair notice as to what the Commission believes Section 5 prohibits or requires."[101] Some had predicted that, if the court had ruled in Wyndham's favor, then, barring any legislative action by Congress, future such lawsuits by the FTC over data security could become more problematic for the independent agency.[102] However, on April 7, 2014, the U.S. District Court for the District of New Jersey denied Wyndham's motion to dismiss the FTC's lawsuit, ruling that the FTC had adequately stated claims that Wyndham engaged in unfair and deceptive practices.[103]

Several bills have been introduced in the Senate in the 113th Congress that could, in varying ways, impact the FTC's powers. S. 1193 (Senator Toomey), S. 1897 (Senator Leahy), S. 1927 (Senator Carper and Senator Blunt), S. 1976 (Senator Rockefeller), and S. 1995 (Senator Blumenthal) would expressly give the FTC the power to levy civil penalties with respect to companies that fail to comply with certain data security standards. S. 1897 would permit the FTC to impose civil penalties for violations for failing to comply with federal cybersecurity standards. S. 1976 would provide the FTC with explicit authority to promulgate "information security" regulations that could extend to certain non-profits. The bill would further allow the FTC to enforce violations of these regulations with various civil penalties. Likewise, S. 1995 would give enforcement authority to the FTC. In several hearings related to the Target breach, some Members of Congress broached the subject of increasing the FTC's powers to pursue data breach actions.[104]

Creating Federal Standards for Data Security, Including for Businesses

Some contend that a federal data breach notification law on its own is insufficient to combat widespread data breaches, primarily because the notification comes after the fact of a breach.[105] Such critics advocate that in addition to data breach notification, the federal government might create standards for what represents a minimum acceptable level of data security. One study noted that a lack of clarity in terms of what precautions businesses should take to protect consumers' personal information has resulted in a patchwork of state data security standards.[106] Though the FTC has proposed some generic guidelines, the agency arguably does not have authority to promulgate official regulations which could detail such standards more fully.[107]

Creating a federal standard for data security has both proponents and opponents in Congress. On the one hand, critics voice concerns that a federal standard would be too rigid for such a rapidly evolving, technology-driven field as data security.[108] They fear that a federal standard could be burdensome and could lag behind new technological trends or even discourage businesses from adopting newer technologies to prevent fraud. On the other hand, proponents of creating federal data security standards argue that such a standard need not be specific nor advocate particular technologies.[109] According to this argument, the federal statute could, for example, consist of a mandate that an organization[110] employ a level of data security that is "reasonable" for the size and complexity of its data operations, for the cost of available tools to reduce vulnerabilities, and for the volume and sensitivity of consumer information it holds.[111]

Bills in both the Senate and the House appear to create differing types of federal standards for data security, along with other changes, such as data breach notification. Bills on this subject include S. 1193, S. 1897, S. 1976, S. 1995, and S. 1927. S. 1193 and H.R. 1468 would require covered entities to "take reasonable measures to protect and secure data in electronic form containing personal information."[112]

Section 202 of S. 1897 and H.R. 3990 would establish broad information security standards and would further authorize the FTC to establish more detailed data security regulations. Such regulations would relate to the implementation of a personal data privacy and security program, vulnerability testing of data security by firms, periodic risk assessments, and employee training on data security.[113] To enforce these data security standards, both bills would provide for civil penalties for violations of the standards.[114]

S. 1927 sets forth a requirement that covered entities "implement, maintain, and enforce reasonable policies and procedures to protect the confidentiality and security of sensitive account information and sensitive personal information.... "[115] Rather than leaving it entirely to the FTC to promulgate rules on these standards, it would give that rulemaking authority, along with enforcement authority, to each institution's prudential regulator.[116] For financial institutions, that prudential regulator would be either the Office of the Comptroller of the Currency (OCC), the Federal Reserve, or the Federal Deposit Insurance Corporation (FDIC). For institutions that are registered investment advisers, investment companies, or broker-dealers, that regulator would be the Securities and Exchange Commission. For institutions that are futures commission merchants, commodity trading advisors, commodity pool operators, or introducing brokers, the regulator would be the Commodity Futures Trading Commission. For Fannie Mae or Freddie Mac, the regulator would be the Federal Housing Finance Agency. For any other business not covered by these categories, the regulator would be the FTC.

S. 1976[117] would authorize the FTC to promulgate regulations providing detailed security standards and would set out four requirements for the FTC to analyze in its rulemaking, along with other requirements, such as a designated officer for information security and a written security policy regarding use and storage of personal information.[118]

S. 1995 would set out requirements for a personal data privacy and security program[119] and would give the FTC the right to promulgate rules further delineating these requirements.[120] The bill requires companies to conduct risk assessments, adopt risk controls, conduct employee training in data security, and conduct periodic vulnerability assessments.[121] It provides enforcement authority, and the right to levy civil penalties, to the Department of Justice, and in some cases, to state attorneys general, and also creates a private right of action.[122]

The executive branch has released a voluntary framework for data security among so-called critical infrastructure industries. On February 12, 2014, the National Institute of Standards and Technology (NIST), an agency within the Department of Commerce, issued its *Framework for Improving Critical Infrastructure Cybersecurity*, known more commonly as *The Cybersecurity Framework*. While the financial sector is considered to be part of the U.S. "critical infrastructure," the retail sector is not.[123] Thus, the "merchants" sector discussed in this report on the Target breach are not included in this voluntary framework. Target, however, owns a bank and after its data breaches used this to become the first retailer to join the financial services information sharing and analysis sector (FS-ISAC).[124] The NIST framework is discussed in more detail in the CRS Legal Sidebar *National Institute of Standards and Technology Issues Long-awaited Cybersecurity Framework*.[125] The impact of the NIST framework remains to be seen.[126] Being voluntary, the framework contains no direct means to enforce compliance. Some have argued, however, that the existence of the framework could potentially create a basis for a standard of conduct that could possibly become a benchmark for courts to evaluate liability relating to data security under tort and other law.[127]

Requiring Adoption of More Advanced Technologies

One issue that has been raised in hearings (but not pursued legislatively) has been the question of how costs for improved cybersecurity—including penalties and fees for breaches—are allocated across merchants, credit card companies, payment processors, and issuing and acquiring banks. This is problematic as customer PII is shared by these companies and must be protected through the payment chain.[128] To use a simple analogy, in a house shared by several roommates, each wants to see the house kept clean, but no one wants to clean the living room. Similarly, customer information is often protected by each of these parties to the payment system at different points along the way, including by the merchant, the payment card company, the issuing and acquiring banks, and the payment processor. This creates a similar problem of participants trying to shift the costs of cyber protection to the other participants.[129] How cybersecurity costs are allocated relates to the question of whether retailers, banks, and payment card companies have been willing to pay for, and adopt, new data security technology quickly enough.

These issues were raised in congressional hearings. Witnesses at times criticized parties representing merchants, banks, or payment card companies for inadequate payment card security, resulting in what the media called "finger-pointing."[130] Yet it is unclear whether a superior legislative solution to this shared property problem exists.[131] Currently, a web of negotiated agreements allocates liability for customer breaches among the various parties. Merchant trade groups, however, have complained that excessive market power of payment card companies, such as MasterCard and Visa, has forced an undue share of the costs of cybersecurity protections on the merchants, and that they also bear an unduly high share of the penalties and indemnifications to payment card companies and banks for breaches, while payment card companies are not spending enough to upgrade security technology, including moving from magnetic stripe and signature to Chip and PIN.[132] Banks, meanwhile, have complained that they pay most of the costs to reissue cards and reimburse for fraudulent charges and that often such breaches result from merchants' security errors.[133]

Could a legislative solution better allocate such costs compared with individually negotiated contracts? A 2010 Federal Reserve Bank of Philadelphia discussion paper[134] interviewed many payment system participants and found that, while merchants have a vested interest in protecting data to uphold their reputations and brands, as well as to avoid chargebacks, some did not feel they had ownership over the fraud mitigation system with which they contractually have to comply.[135] One concern voiced by banks and payment card companies was that if data security were to become a competitive factor, information sharing and cooperating on data security might be more difficult.[136] Consumers might view competition for superior data security as desirable. While the article raised questions such as to whether the costs of payment card fraud and of avoiding such fraud are borne by the appropriate parties in the payment system, it concluded only that, "The answers to these questions are not simple."[137]

A number of Members of Congress participating in the Target hearings raised the question of why the United States still had not moved to a Chip and PIN system (see "What Industry Best Practices Have Been Adopted?" for more information), as this technology is widely believed to make breaches more difficult.[138] Senator Warren pressed industry representatives to explain why they had not yet adopted this Chip and PIN technology, and she suggested that government action might be warranted to encourage adoption of new technology.[139] Senator Durbin stated that retailers and customers were actually paying one cent for each transaction to cover anti-fraud and security costs of payment cards, and questioned whether the technology upgrades were being adopted quickly enough, in light of this.[140] But, while Members raised the question often of why more advanced technology had not yet been adopted in America, in contrast to the European Chip and PIN standard, they generally stopped short of advocating that the federal government mandate any specific technology upgrades or changes at this point in time.

GLOSSARY

Table 2. Glossary of Terms

Terms	Explanation
acquirer	The acquirer is the financial institution used by a merchant in a payment card transaction.
cardholder	A cardholder is the person having a payment card.
Chip and PIN	Chip and PIN is a payment card security system with an embedded microprocessor chip and requiring a personal identification number.
Chip and Signature	Chip and Signature is a payment card security system with an embedded microprocessor chip and requiring the cardholder's signature
clearing	Clearing is the process of settling a payment card transaction.
discount rate	The discount rate is the rate charged a merchant by its acquiring bank for processing.
EMV	EMV is a chip standard originally created by Europay, MasterCard, and Visa. It is used in chip-based systems around the world.
encryption	Encryption is using a computer program to scramble information into cipher text so that it makes no sense.
interchange fee	The interchange fee is the fee charged by a payment card for its role in processing a transaction. It is deducted from the funds paid by the issuer to the acquirer.
issuer	The issuer is the bank or other financial institution that issues a payment card to the cardholder.
merchant	A merchant is the organization selling goods or services and accepting a payment card.
payment card	A payment card is a credit card, debit card, prepaid card, or ATM card.
PCI Council	PCI Council is the Payment Card Industry Council, a standards setting group.

Table 2. (Continued)

Terms	Explanation
PCI DSS	PCI DSS is an acronym for Payment Card Industry data security standards. Currently at version 3.0.
PII	PII is an acronym for personally identifiable information.
PIN	PIN is an acronym for personal identification number, used to authenticate a cardholder in a financial transaction.
POS	POS is an acronym for point of sale, which frequently refers to the machine that reads a payment card.
payment processor	A payment processor is a company that connects a merchant with an acquiring bank in a payment card transaction. Payment processors can establish an account with an acquirer for a merchant.
tokenization	Tokenization is replacing a payment card account number with another number.

Source: The Congressional Research Service.

APPENDIX. LOSS CALCULATIONS OF POTENTIAL LOSSES IN TARGET DATA BREACH

Table A-1. Jefferies Calculations

	Highest Volume Issuers	Other Issuers	Total
Cards compromised			
Card issuers	80%	20%	100%
Compromised cards (millions)	32 million	8 million	40 million
Percentage of cards with fraudulent charges			
Low estimate	10%	20%	
High estimate	15%	30%	
Resulting number of cards with fraudulent charges			
Low estimate	3.2 million[a]	1.6 million[a]	4.8 million
High estimate	4.8 million[a]	2.4 million[a]	7.2 million
Potential fraud assuming $300 per card			
Low estimate	$960 million[a]	$480 million[a]	$1,440 million[a]

Highest Volume Issuers	Other Issuers	Total	
High estimate	$1,440 million[a]	$720 million[a]	$2,160 million[a]
Potential PCI fines			
Fine at 30% of estimated fraud	$288 million[a]	$144 million[a]	$432 million
Fine at 50% of estimated fraud	$720 million[a]	$360 million[a]	$1,080 million

Source: Daniel Binder, "Jefferies Equity Research, Americas: Target," January 29, 2014. The company credits the estimates to conversations with Julie Conroy of Aite Group, a payment cards industry expert. The names of the highest volume issuers are not given.

a. Designates calculations done by CRS using methodology reported in Daniel Binder, "Jefferies Equity Research, Americas: Target," January 29, 2014.

Table A-2. Calculations Using Visa and Jefferies Assumptions

Cards compromised	
Compromised cards (all brands)	40 million
Visa estimates of percentage of cards with fraudulent charges	
Low estimate	2%
High estimate	5%
Number of cards with fraudulent charges	
Low estimate	800,000
High estimate	2 million
Potential fraud assuming $300 per card	
Low estimate	$240 million
High estimate	$600 million
Potential PCI fines	
Low estimate	$72 million
High estimate	$300 million

Sources: Daniel Binder, "Jefferies Equity Research, Americas: Target," January 29, 2014; Testimony of Ellen Richey, Chief Enterprise Risk Officer, Visa, Inc. before U.S. Congress, Senate Committee on Commerce, Science, and Transportation, *Hearing on Protecting Personal Consumer Information from Cyber Attacks and Data Breaches*, 113th Cong., 2nd sess., March 26, 2014, p. 12, at http://www.commerce.senate.gov/public/?a=Files.Serve&File_id=9d2d04c0-0aa2-4a07-9a11-81d74a7339a8.

Note: Calculations use Visa's estimates of the percentage of cards with fraudulent charges and Jefferies' estimate of $300 of fraud for each card used fraudulently.

End Notes

[1] Testimony of John J. Mulligan, executive vice president and chief financial officer, Target, before U.S. Congress, Senate, Committee on Commerce, Science, and Transportation, *Protecting Personal Consumer Information from Cyber Attacks and Data Breaches*, 113th Cong., 2nd sess., March 26, 2014, at http://www.commerce.senate.gov/public/?a=Files.Serve&File_id=c2103bd3-8c40-42c3-973b-bd08c7de45ef; U.S. Congress, Senate, Committee on the Judiciary, *Privacy in the Digital Age: Preventing Data Breaches and Combating Cybercrime*, 113th Cong., 2nd sess., February 4, 2014, at http://www.judiciary.senate.gov/pdf/02-04-14MulliganTestimony.pdf, and U.S. Congress, House of Representatives, Committee on Energy and Commerce, Subcommittee on Commerce, Manufacturing, and Trade, *Protecting Consumer Information: Can Data Breaches Be Prevented?*, 113th Cong., 2nd sess., February 5, 2014, at http://docs.house.gov/meetings/IF/IF17/20140205/101714/HMTG-113-IF17-Wstate-MulliganJ-20140205.pdf.

[2] Hilary Stout, "Target Vows to Speed Anti-Fraud Technology," *New York Times*, February 4, 2014, at http://www.nytimes.com/2014/02/05/business/target-to-speed-adoption-of-european-anti-fraud-technology.html.

[3] Jennifer Bjorhus, "Banks Have Replaced 15.3 Million Cards since Target Breach," *Minneapolis Star Tribune*, January 29, 2014, at http://www.startribune.com/business/242505661.html, and Nathaniel Popper, "Theft at Target Leads Citi to Replace Debit Cards," *New York Times*, January 16, 2014, p. B3, New York, at http://www.nytimes.com/2014/01/16/business/theft-at-target-leads-citi-to-replace-debit-cards.html?_r=0.

[4] Target Corporation, "Form 10-K," Fiscal Year Ended February 2, 2013, p. 17, at http://edgar.sec.gov/Archives/edgar/data/27419/000104746913003100/a2213506z10-k.htm#da18701_part_i.

[5] Ibid., p. 17.

[6] Daniel Binder, "Jefferies Equity Research, Americas: Target," January 29, 2014. Jefferies credits the estimates to conversations with Julie Conroy of Aite Group, a payment cards industry expert.

[7] When the card is not present, the acquiring bank is responsible, but can seek to recovery from the merchant. See Randall Stross, "$9 Here, 20 Cents There and a Credit-Card Lawsuit," *New York Times*, August 22, 2010, p. BU3, New York edition, at http://www.nytimes.com/2010/08/22/business/22digi.html?_r=1&src=me&ref=business.

[8] Testimony of Ellen Richey, Chief Enterprise Risk Officer, Visa, Inc. before U.S. Congress, Senate Committee on Commerce, Science, and Transportation, *Hearing on Protecting Personal Consumer Information from Cyber Attacks and Data Breaches*, 113th Cong., 2nd sess., March 26, 2014, p. 12, at http://www.commerce.senate.gov/public/?a=Files.Serve&File_id=9d2d04c0-0aa2-4a07-9a11-81d74a7339a8.

[9] Target, "Form 8-K," February 26, 2014, at http://edgar.sec.gov/Archives/edgar/data/27419/000002741914000006/ a2013q48k.htm.

[10] Testimony of John J. Mulligan, executive vice president and chief financial officer, Target, before U.S. Congress, Senate, Committee on Commerce, Science, and Transportation, *Protecting Personal Consumer Information from Cyber Attacks and Data Breaches*, 113th Cong., 2nd sess., March 26, 2014, p. 5, at http://www.commerce.senate.gov/public/?a=Files.Serve&File_id=c2103bd3-8c40-42c3-973b-bd08c7de45ef.

[11] Fazio Mechanical Services, "Statement on Target Data Breach," press release, at http://faziomechanical.com/Target-Breach-Statement.pdf. Target has not publicly identified the vendor.

[12] A POS system includes a cash register, payment card terminal, and related computer hardware and software. More sophisticated systems can monitor inventory and produce various business reports.

[13] Brian Krebs, "Email Attack on Vendor Set up Breach at Target," *Krebs on Security*, February 14, 2014, at https://krebsonsecurity.com/2014/02/email-attack-on-vendor-set-up-breach-at-target/.

[14] Jim Finkle and Mark Hosenball, "Exclusive: FBI Warns Retailers to Expect More Credit Card Breaches," *Reuters*, January 23, 2014, at http://www.reuters.com/article/2014/01/24/us-target-databreach-fbi-idUSBREA0M1UF20140124.

[15] Nicole Perlroth, "Latest Sites of Breaches in Security Are Hotels," *New York Times*, January 31, 2014, p. B4, New York Edition, at http://www.nytimes.com/2014/02/01/technology/latest-sites-of-breaches-in-security-are-hotels.html.

[16] For a more detailed report on the Target breach, see U.S. Congress, Senate, Committee on Commerce, Science, and Transportation, *A "Kill Chain" Analysis of the 2013 Target Data Breach: Majority Staff Report for Chairman Rockefeller*, March 26, 2014, at http://www.commerce.senate.gov/public/?a=Files.Serve&File_id=24d3c229-4f2f-405d-b8db-a3a67f183883.

[17] According to BloombergBusinessweek, Target security specialists in Bangalore detected the malware and reported the problem to Target's headquarters security, which did nothing. See Michael Riley, Ben Elgin, and Dune Lawrence, et al., "Missed Alarms and 40 Million Stolen Credit Card Numbers: How Target Blew It," *BloombergBusinessweek*, March 13, 2014, at http://www.businessweek.com/articles/2014-03-13/target-missed-alarms-in-epic-hack-of-credit-card-data#p1.

[18] The term "four-party" is a bit misleading because it does not count the payment network (also called the network provider), e.g., the credit or debit card company.

[19] This fee is called the merchant discount fee.

[20] "Purchase Volume for U.S. General Purpose Brands," *Nilson Report*, February 2014.

[21] For contrasting views, see Testimony of Mallory Duncan, General Council, National Retail Federation, before U.S. Congress, Senate Committee on Banking, Housing, and Urban Affairs, Subcommittee on National Security and International Trade and Finance, *Safeguarding Consumers' Financial Data*, 113th Cong., 2nd sess., February 3, 2014; and Clint Boulton, "Retail Association: Card Security Costs Outweigh Benefits for Many," *Wall Street Journal: CIO Journal*, March 26, 2014, at http://blogs.wsj.com/cio/2014/03/26/retail-association-card-security-costs-outweigh-benefits-for-many/.

[22] A POS system includes a cash register, payment card terminal, and related computer hardware and software. More sophisticated systems can monitor inventory and produce various business reports.

[23] David Morrison, "Visa Emphasizing that New Cards Will Not Need Offline PINs," *Credit Union Times*, January 16, 2012, at http://www.cutimes.com/2012/01/16/visa-emphasizing-that-new-cards-will-not-need-offl. It is not clear how chip-based systems without payment network access can be kept up-to-date for credit limit availability.

[24] MasterCard, "Progress against Roadmap," June 20, 2013, at http://www.mastercard.us/_assets/docs/ MasterCard_EMV_Timeline.pdf.

[25] EMV Connection, "U.S. EMV Issuers," at http://www.emv-connection.com/u-s-emv-issuers/. Issuers listed are AAA Visa, American Express, Andrews Federal Credit Union, Bank of America, Diners Club Chase, Citi, North Carolina State Employees' Credit Union, PSCU Financial Services, Silicon Valley Bank, Star One Credit Union, State Employees Credit Union, SunTrust, Travelex Cash Passport, United Nations Federal Credit Union, U.S. Bank, and Wells Fargo.

[26] EMV, "Worldwide EMV Deployment and Adoption," Q4 2012, at http://www.emvco.com/documents/EMVCo_EMV_Deployment_Stats1.pdf.

[27] Sharon Guadin, "Security Breaches Cost $90 to $305 Per Lost Record," *InformationWeek*, March 3, 2007, at http://www.informationweek.com/security-breaches-cost-$90-to-$305-per-lost-record/d/d-id/1053922?.

[28] Symantec and Ponemon Institute, "Databreach Calculator: Estimate Your Risk Exposure," at https://databreachcalculator.com/Calculator/Default.aspx.

[29] Ponemon Institute, "2013 Cost of Data Breach Study: United States," p. 6, at http://www.symantec.com/content/en/us/about/media/pdfs/b-cost-of-a-data-breach-us-report-2013.en-us.pdf?om_ext_cid=biz_socmed_twitter_facebook_marketwire_linkedin_2013Jun_worldwide_CostofaDataBreach. The Ponemon Institute's estimates are based on a non-random sample of 54 companies and include all breaches, not just those targeting payment cards.

[30] Target, "Target Reports Fourth Quarter and Full-Year 2013 Earnings," press release, February 26, 2014, at http://investors.target.com/phoenix.zhtml?c=65828&p=irol-newsArticle&ID=1903678&highlight=.

[31] Walmart, "Walmart reports Q4 underlying EPS of $1.60, Fiscal 2014 underlying EPS of $5.11," press release, at http://media.corporate-ir.net/media_files/IROL/11/112761/FY14Q4EarningsReleasefinal.pdf.

[32] Costco Wholesale Corporation, "Costco Wholesale Corporation Reports December Sales Results," press release, January 5, 2014, at http://phx.corporate-ir.net/phoenix.zhtml?c=83830&p=irol-newsArticle&ID=1889295&highlight=.

[33] See for example, Independent Community Bankers of America, "Community Banks Reissue More Than 4 Million Payment Cards Following Retailer Data Breaches," press release, February 19, 2014, at http://www.icba.org/news/newsreleasedetail.cfm?itemnumber=178594&pf=1.

[34] Global Payments, "Form 10-K for the Fiscal Year Ended May 31, 2013," p. 62, at http://www.sec.gov/Archives/ edgar/data/1123360/000112336013000025/gpn20130531-10k.htm. Visa has been publicly identified as one of the cards that suspended Global Payments. See Jessica Silver-Greenberg, "After a Data Breach, Visa Removes a Service Provider," *New York Times*, April 2, 2012, p. B6, New York edition, at http://www.nytimes.com/2012/04/02/business/after-data-breach-visa-removes-a-service-provider.html?_r=1&emc=tnt&tntemail0=y.

[35] Tracy Kitten, "Global Closes Breach Investigation: Processor Says Expenses Less than Originally Reported," *Bank Info Security*, April 15, 2013, at http://www.bankinfosecurity.com/global-closes-breach-investigation-a-5684/op-1.

[36] Federal Trade Commission, "Lost or Stolen Credit, ATM, and Debit Cards," at http://www.consumer.ftc.gov/articles/ 0213-lost-or-stolen-credit-atm-and-debit-cards.

[37] For more on this, see Ryan Tracy, "In a Cyber Breach, Who Pays, Banks or Retailers?; The Theft of Personal and Card Data at Target Has Rekindled Debate," *Wall Street Journal*, January 12, 2014, at http://online.wsj.com/news/ articles/SB10001424052702303819704579316861842957106 and Tom Webb, "Analysts See Target Breach Costs Topping $1 Billion," *St. Paul Pioneer Press*, February 21, 2014, at http://www.twincities.com/business/ci_25029900/ analyst-sees-target-data-breach-costs-topping-1.

[38] See First Choice Federal Credit Union v. Target, U.S. District Court for the Western District of Pennsylvania, Complaint filed January 31, 2014. For an overview, see Joel Schectman, "Banks Heap Suits on Target over Breach," *Wall Street Journal*, February 7, 2014, at http://blogs.wsj.com/riskandcompliance/2014/02/07/banks-heap-suits-on-target-over-data-breach/.

[39] First Choice Federal Credit Union v. Target, U.S. District Court for the Western District of Pennsylvania, Complaint filed January 31, 2014, p. 2.

[40] Michael Riley, Ben Elgin, and Dune Lawrence et al., "Missed Alarms and 40 Million Stolen Credit Card Numbers: How Target Blew It," *BloombergBusinessweek*, March 13, 2014, at http://www.businessweek.com/articles/2014-03-13/ target-missed-alarms-in-epic-hack-of-credit-card-data#p1.

[41] See, e.g., Michael Riley, Ben Elgin, and Dune Lawrence et al., "Missed Alarms and 40 Million Stolen Credit Card Numbers: How Target Blew It," *BloombergBusinessweek*, March 13, 2014, at http://www.businessweek.com/articles/ 2014-03-13/target-missed-alarms-in-epic-hack-of-credit-card-data#p1. This call has been echoed by academics. For example, see. Richard A. Epstein and Thomas P. Brown "Cybersecurity in the Payment Card Industry,"

The University of Chicago Law Review, vol. 75, no. 1 (winter, 2008), pp. 203-223, which notes, " ... of equal importance is the allocation of losses among innocent parties who have suffered losses from various forms of theft," see http://www.jstor.org/stable/20141905.

[42] See Richard A. Epstein and Thomas P. Brown "Cybersecurity in the Payment Card Industry," *The University of Chicago Law Review*, vol. 75, no. 1 (winter, 2008), p. 206.

[43] PCI Security Standards Council, "PCI Data Storage Do's and Don'ts," October, 2008, at https://www.pcisecuritystandards.org/pdfs/pci_fs_data_storage.pdf. The service code specifies acceptance requirements and limitations on the card.

[44] PCI Security Standards Council, "Data Security Standard: Requirements and Security Assessment Procedures," Version 3.0, November 2013, p. 5, at https://www.pcisecurity standards.org/security_standards/documents.php.

[45] Lisa Eadiccio and James Fanelli, "Not Much to Forging a Counterfeit Credit Card, Technology is Readily Available," *Daily News*, February 3, 2011, at http://www.nydailynews.com/ news/forging-counterfeit-credit-card-technology-readily-article-1.133144?print.

[46] Testimony of Mallory Duncan, General Council, National Retail Federation, before U.S. Congress, Senate, Committee on Banking, Housing, and Urban Affairs, Subcommittee on National Security and International Trade and Finance, *Safeguarding Consumers' Financial Data*, 113th Cong., 2nd sess., February 3, 2014.

[47] For example, Clint Boulton, "Retail Association: Card Security Costs Outweigh Benefits for Many," *Wall Street Journal: CIO Journal*, March 26, 2014, at http://blogs.wsj.com/cio/ 2014/03/26/retail-association-card-security-costs-outweigh-benefits-for-many/.

[48] Mike Bond, Omar Choudary, and Steven J. Murdoch, et al., *Chip and Skim: Cloning EMV Cards with the Pre-Play Attack*, Computer Laboratory, University of Cambridge, UK, at http://www.cl.cam.ac.uk/~rja14/Papers/unattack.pdf. See, also, Mike Bond, "Chip and Skim: Cloning EMV Cards with the Pre-Play Attack," *Light Blue Touchpaper*, September 10, 2012, at http://www.lightbluetouchpaper.org/2012/09/10/chip-and-skim-cloning-emv-cards-with-the-pre-play-attack/, and Steven J. Murdoch and Ross Anderson, "Security Protocols and Evidence: Where Many Payment Systems Fail," Financial Cryptography and Data Security 2014, March 2014, at http://www.cl.cam.ac.uk/~sjm217/papers/ fc14evidence.pdf.

[49] Testimony of Fran Rosch, Senior Vice President Security Product and Services, Endpoint and Mobility, Symantec Corporation, before U.S. Congress, Senate Committee on the Judiciary, *Hearing on Privacy in the Digital Age: Preventing Data Breaches and Combating Cybercrime*, 113th Cong., 2nd sess., February 4, 2014.

[50] Visa, *Visa U.S. Merchant EMV Chip Acceptance Readiness Guide*, June 2013, p. 4, at http://usa.visa.com/download/merchants/visa-merchant-chip-acceptance-readiness-guide. pdf.

[51] Danielle Douglas, "MasterCard, Visa Explain Why Your Credit Card Isn't Safer," *Washington Post*, February 20, 2014, at http://www.washingtonpost.com/blogs/wonkblog/wp/2014/02/ 20/mastercard-visa-explain-why-your-credit-card-isnt-safer/.

[52] Dune Lawrence, "Hack-Resistant Credit Cards Bring More Safety—at a Price," *BloombergBusinessweek*, February 14, 2014, at http://www.businessweek.com/articles/ 2014-02-14/hack-resistant-credit-cards-bring-greater-security-at-a-big-price.

[53] Testimony of Mallory Duncan, General Council, National Retail Federation, before U.S. Congress, Senate Committee on Banking, Housing, and Urban Affairs, Subcommittee on National Security and International Trade and Finance, *Safeguarding Consumers' Financial Data*, 113th Cong., 2nd sess., February 3, 2014.

[54] A web search found many vendors (including Amazon.com) selling POS payment card readers for approximately $300.

[55] First Data, *Avoiding a Data Breach: An Introduction to Encryption and Tokenization*, 2013, at http://files.firstdata.com/downloads/thought-leadership/6203-Data-Breach-Market-Insight. pdf and First Data, *What Data Thieves Don't Want You to Know: The Facts about*

Encryption and Tokenization. A First Data White Paper, 2012, at http://files.firstdata.com/downloads/thought-leadership/TokenizationEncryptionWP.pdf.

[56] First Data, *Avoiding a Data Breach: An Introduction to Encryption and Tokenization*, 2013, at http://files.firstdata.com/downloads/thought-leadership/6203-Data-Breach-Market-Insight.pdf and First Data, *What Data Thieves Don't Want You to Know: The Facts about Encryption and Tokenization. A First Data White Paper*, 2012, at http://files.firstdata.com/downloads/thought-leadership/TokenizationEncryptionWP.pdf.

[57] The Federal Reserve has defined mobile banking as "accessing your bank's web page through the web browser on your mobile phone, via text messaging, or by using an application downloaded to your mobile phone." See Board of Governors of the Federal Reserve System, "Consumers and Mobile Financial Services 2013," March 2013, p. 15, at http://www.federalreserve.gov/econresdata/consumers-and-mobile-financial-services-report-201303.pdf. The report defines mobile payments similarly and includes payments made by telephone bill, credit card bill, or directly from a bank account. The definition could be expanded to include tablets.

[58] These hearings included U.S. Congress, Senate Committee on Banking, Housing, and Urban Affairs, Subcommittee on National Security and International Trade and Finance, Safeguarding Consumers' Financial Data, 113th Cong., 2nd sess., February 3, 2014 and, *Oversight of Financial Stability and Data Security*, February 6, 2014; 113th Cong., 2nd sess., at http://www.banking.senate.gov/public/index.cfm?FuseAction=Hearings.Hearing&Hearing_ID=8a669045-f9b9-4c7e-b1df-1bb08e694e90, U.S. Congress, Senate, Committee on the Judiciary, *Privacy in the Digital Age: Preventing Data Breaches and Combating Cybercrime*, February 4, 2014; 113th Cong., 2nd sess., at http://www.judiciary.senate.gov/hearings/hearing.cfm?id=138603a26950ad873303535a6300170f; U.S. Congress, House of Representatives, Committee on Energy and Commerce Committee, *Protecting Consumer Information: Can Data Breaches Be Prevented?*, 113th Cong., 2nd sess., February 5, 2014; at http://energycommerce.house.gov/hearing/ protecting-consumer-information-can-data-breaches-be-prevented, the House Financial Services Committee, Subcommittee on Financial Institutions and Consumer Credit, *Data Security: Examining Efforts to Protect Americans' Financial Information*, March 5, 2014, at http://energycommerce.house.gov/hearing/protecting-consumer-information-can-data-breaches-be-prevented, and U.S. Congress, Senate, Committee on Commerce, *Protecting Personal Consumer Information from Cyber Attacks and Data Breaches*, 113th Cong., 2nd sess., March 26, 2014, at http://www.commerce.senate.gov/public/index.cfm?p=Hearings&ContentRecord_id=082407f8-9740-4e43-b2d2-1520c5495014&ContentType_id=14f995b9-dfa5-407a-9d35-56cc7152a7ed&Group_id=b06c39af-e033-4cba-9221-de668ca1978a; U.S. Congress, Senate Committee on Homeland Security and Governmental Affairs, *Data Breach on the Rise: Protecting Personal Information from Harm*, 113th Cong., 2nd sess., April 2, 2014, at http://www.hsgac.senate.gov/hearings/data-breach-on-the-rise-protecting-personal-information-from-harm.

[59] For detailed background and information on data breach notification laws, including details on states' laws, please see CRS Report R42475, *Data Security Breach Notification Laws*, by Gina Stevens. For additional background and information on prior bills introducing a federal data breach notification standard, please see CRS Report R42474, *Selected Federal Data Security Breach Legislation*, by Kathleen Ann Ruane. For an update on the number of states with such laws, see National Conference of State Legislatures, "State Security Breach Notification Laws," April 11, 2014, at http://www.ncsl.org/research/telecommunications-and-information-technology/security-breach-notification-laws.aspx.

[60] CRS Report R42475, *Data Security Breach Notification Laws*, by Gina Stevens.

[61] CRS Report R42474, *Selected Federal Data Security Breach Legislation*, by Kathleen Ann Ruane.

[62] 15 U.S.C. §§6801-6809.

[63] 42 U.S.C. §1320d et seq.

[64] P.L. 111-5.

[65] In addition to certain financial institutions and healthcare facilities, the FTC enforces several statutes and rules imposing obligations upon some businesses that collect and maintain consumer data. This includes the Children's Online Privacy Protection Act (COPPA) (15 U.S.C. §§6501-6506), which requires reasonable security for children's information collected online. Also, the Fair Credit Reporting Act (FCRA) requires consumer reporting agencies to use reasonable procedures to ensure that those to whom they disclose sensitive information have a permissible purpose for it. Nevertheless, only a few segments of the private economy are subject to any data security requirements, much less data breach notification requirements. See "Prepared Statement Of The Federal Trade Commission" before U.S. Congress, House of Representatives, The Committee On Energy And Commerce Subcommittee On Commerce, Manufacturing, And Trade, *Protecting Consumer Information: Can Data Breaches Be Prevented?*, February 5, 2014, at http://docs.house.gov/meetings/IF/IF17/20140205/101714/HMTG-113-IF17-Wstate-RamirezE-20140205.pdf.

[66] For more on this, please see CRS Legal Sidebar, *Federal Securities Laws and Recent Data Breaches*.

[67] National Conference of State Legislatures, "State Security Breach Notification Laws," April 11, 2014, at http://www.ncsl.org/research/telecommunications-and-information-technology/security-breach-notification-laws.aspx. For a discussion of the differences in state data breach notification laws, see Reid J. Schar and Kathleen W. Gibbons, "Complicated Compliance: State Data Breach Notification Laws," *Bloomberg BNA*, August 9, 2013, at http://www.bna.com/complicated-compliance-state-data-breach-notification-laws/. For summaries of state data breach notification laws, see Perkins Cole, "Security Breach Notification Chart," October 2013, at http://www.perkinscoie.com/statebreachchart/ and Mintz, Levin, Cohn, Ferris, Glovsky & Popeo, P.C. "State Data Breach Notification Laws," December 1, 2013, at http://www.mintz.com/newsletter/2007/PrivSec-DataBreachLaws-02-07/state_data_breach_matrix.pdf.

[68] National Conference of State Legislatures, "State Security Breach Notification Laws," April 11, 2014, at http://www.ncsl.org/research/telecommunications-and-information-technology/security-breach-notification-laws.aspx.

[69] Cal. Civ. Code §§1798.29, 1798.80 et seq.

[70] These state laws can have differing or conflicting requirements, as well. For instance, some states require immediate notification, while others, such as Ohio and Wisconsin, require notification within 45 days. For a side-by-side summary of the data breach notification requirements of the state laws, please see Scott & Scott, "State Data Breach Notification Laws," Sept. 21, 2007, at http://www.scottandscottllp.com/resources/state_data_breach_notification_law.pdf.

[71] For instance, see Testimony of James Reuter, President of First Data Corp., before U.S. Congress, Senate, Committee on Banking, Housing, and Urban Affairs, Subcommittee on National Security and International Trade and Finance, *Safeguarding Consumers' Financial Data*, 113th Cong., 2nd sess., February 3, 2014, "Consumers' electronic payments are not confined by borders between states. As such, a national standard for data security breach notification, as contained in Senate bill 1927, the Data Security Act of 2014, is of paramount importance." The National Retail Federation and the Financial Services Roundtable, among other business groups, have echoed the call for a national data breach notification law. For such calls from academics, see, e.g., Tom, Jacqueline May, "A Simple Compromise: The Need for a Federal Data Breach Notification Law," 84 *St. John's Law Review* 1569 (2010); Winn, Jane K., Are "Better" Security Breach Notification Laws Possible?" *Berkley Technology Law Journal*, vol. 24, June 8, 2009, at http://ssrn.com/abstract=1416222.

[72] National Retail Federation, Financial Services Roundtable, et al., "Merchant and Financial Trade Associations Announce Cybersecurity Partnership," press release, February 13, 2014,

at http://nrf.com/modules.php?name= Documents&op=showlivedoc&sp_id=7818 or at http://fsroundtable.org/merchant-and-financial-trade-associations-announce-cybersecurity-partnership/.

[73] Testimony of Edmund Mierzwinski, Director, Consumer Program, U.S. Public Interest Research Group, before U.S. Congress, Senate, Committee on Banking, Housing and Urban Affairs, Subcommittee on National Security and International Trade and Finance, *Safeguarding Consumers' Financial Data*, Panel 2," February 3, 2014, at http://www.banking.senate.gov/public/index.cfm?FuseAction=Files.View&FileStore_id=3d7b11bb-d07c-41b2-9431-2cf39af48920 and http://www.cq.com/doc/congressionaltranscripts-4417795.

[74] Ibid. Mierzwinski stated, for instance, that he hoped any data breach notification law would trigger notification when personal data had been wrongfully acquired, rather than when actual harm had occurred to consumers.

[75] See, e.g., National Retail Federation, Financial Services Roundtable, et al., "Merchant and Financial Trade Associations Announce Cybersecurity Partnership," press release, February 13, 2014, at http://nrf.com/modules.php? name=Documents&op=showlivedoc&sp_id=7818 or at http://fsroundtable.org/merchant-and-financial-trade-associations-announce-cybersecurity-partnership/.

[76] U.S. Department of Justice, "Attorney General Holder Urges Congress to Create National Standard for Reporting Cyberattacks," press release, February 24, 2014, at http://www.justice.gov/opa/pr/2014/February/14-ag-194.html.

[77] Rob Margetta, "Data Breach Response May Be Limited to Notification," *Roll Call*, March 12, 2014, at http://www.rollcall.com/news/data_breach_response_may_be_limited_to_notification-231430-1.html?zkPrintable= true.

[78] CRS Report R42475, *Data Security Breach Notification Laws*, by Gina Stevens.

[79] H.R. 1468 is a companion bill to S. 1193, and H.R. 3990 is a companion bill to S. 1897.

[80] As discussed later in this section, bills such as S. 1193, S. 1897, S. 1927, S. 1976 and S. 1995 address providing the FTC with additional statutory authorities in various ways.

[81] See e.g., Patricia Cave, "Giving Consumers a Leg to Stand On," *Catholic University Law Review*, Spring 2013, p. 781; and John A. Fisher, "Secure My Data or Pay the Price: Consumer Remedy for the Negligent Enablement of Data Breach," *William & Mary Business Law Review*, 2013, at http://scholarship.law.wm.edu/wmblr/vol4/iss1/7.

[82] 15 U.S.C. §45.

[83] See Testimony of Federal Trade Commission before U.S. Congress, House of Representatives, Committee on Energy and Commerce, Subcommittee on Commerce, Manufacturing, and Trade, *Protecting Consumer Information: Can Data Breaches Be Prevented?* 113th Cong., 2nd sess., February 5, 2014, p. 3.

[84] Ibid.

[85] Ibid.

[86] Ibid.

[87] Ibid., p. 4.

[88] Ibid., p. 11.

[89] Jill Joerling, "Data Breach Notification Laws: An Argument for a Comprehensive Federal Law to Protect Consumer Data," *Washington University Journal of Law and Policy*, vol. 32 (2010), p. 485.

[90] TRENDnet, Inc., No. 122-3090 (September 4, 2013), at http://www.ftc.gov/opa/2013/09/trendnet.shtm.

[91] Testimony of Federal Trade Commission before U.S. Congress, House of Representatives, Committee on Energy and Commerce, Subcommittee on Commerce, Manufacturing, and Trade, *Protecting Consumer Information: Can Data Breaches Be Prevented?*, 113th Cong., 2nd sess., February 5, 2014, p. 6.

[92] Ibid.

[93] *Prepared Statement of the Federal Trade Commission on Data Breach on the Rise: Protecting Personal Information from Harm,* Before the Committee on Homeland Security and Governmental Affairs, United States Senate, April 2, 2014, p. 10: "Under current laws, the FTC only has authority to seek civil penalties for data security violations with regard to children's online information under COPPA or credit report information under the FCRA. To help ensure effective deterrence, we urge Congress to allow the FTC to seek civil penalties for all data security and breach notice violations in appropriate circumstances," at http://www.ftc.gov/system/files/documents/public_statements/296011/140402datasecurity.pdf.

[94] Ibid., p. 11.

[95] Ibid.

[96] Ibid.

[97] Federal Trade Commission v. Wyndham Worldwide Corporation et al., No. 13-1887 (D. N.J. filed March 26, 2013).

[98] Jessica Meyers and Erin Mershon, "Critical Breach Verdict Nears in FTC Case," *Politico*, February 24, 2014.

[99] Ibid.

[100] Notice of Motion to Dismiss by Defendants, Federal Trade Commission v. Wyndham Worldwide Corporation et al., No. 13-1887 (D. N.J. Apr. 26, 2013) ECF No. 91.

[101] Ibid.

[102] See "FTC Administrative Complaint Asserts Authority to Regulate Data Security Practices," *Tech Law Journal*, August 29, 2013, at http://www.techlawjournal.com/topstories/2013/20130829.asp; Jessica Meyers and Erin Mershon, "Critical Breach Verdict Nears in FTC Case," *Politico*, February 24, 2014; and Allison Grande, "FTC Unfairness Authority Designed To Be Broad, Brill Says," *Law 360*, February 19, 2014.

[103] Opinion, Federal Trade Commission v. Wyndham Worldwide Corporation et al., No. 13-1887 (D. N.J. Apr. 7, 2014). The court has not yet ruled on the merits of the FTC's claims at this stage.

[104] See, for example, the comments of Senator Elizabeth Warren during questions and answers during the U.S. Congress, Senate, Banking, Housing, and Urban Affairs Committee hearing *Safeguarding Consumers' Financial Data,* February 3, 2014, Panel 1: "I think this is a real problem, that the FTC's enforcement authority in this area is so limited. The FTC should have the enforcement authority it needs to protect consumers, and it looks like to me it doesn't have that authority right now," at http://www.cq.com/doc/congressionaltranscripts-4417727.

[105] See, e.g., Patricia Cave, "Giving Consumers a Leg to Stand On," *Catholic University Law Review*, Spring 2013, p. 781; and John A. Fisher, "Secure My Data or Pay the Price: Consumer Remedy for the Negligent Enablement of Data Breach," *William & Mary Business Law Review*, 2013, at http://scholarship.law.wm.edu/wmblr/vol4/iss1/7.

[106] Jill Joerling, "Data Breach Notification Laws: An Argument for a Comprehensive Federal Law to Protect Consumer Data," *Washington University Journal of Law and Policy*, vol. 32 (2010), p. 485.

[107] Ibid.

[108] See, e.g., Opening Statement as Prepared, of Representative Lee Terry, Chair of Subcommittee on Commerce Manufacturing and Trade, U.S. Congress, House of Representatives, Committee on Energy and Commerce, Subcommittee on Commerce, Manufacturing, and Trade, Protecting *Consumer Information: Can Data Breaches Be Prevented?*, 113th Cong., 2nd sess., February 5, 2014, at http://energycommerce.house.gov/sites/republicans.energycommerce.house.gov/files/Hearings/CMT/20140205/HHRG-113-IF17-IF03-MState-T000459-20140205.pdf, "I do not believe that we can solve this whole problem by codifying detailed, technical standards or with overly cumbersome mandates. Flexibility, quickness, and nimbleness are all attributes that are absolutely necessary in

cyber security but run contrary to government's abilities.... The security of data itself is paramount in this conversation, but as I have said, cumbersome statutory mandates can be ill equipped to deal with evolving threats. Nonetheless, I think this subcommittee would benefit from hearing about how companies are dealing with this issue now, as well as in the future."

[109] See, e.g., Senator John D. Rockefeller IV, Chairman of the Senate Committee on Commerce, Science, and Transportation, "Rockefeller, Feinstein, Pryor, Nelson Introduce Data Security Bill to Protect Consumers from Data Breaches," press release, January 30, 2014, at http://www.commerce.senate.gov/public/index.cfm?p=PressReleases&ContentRecord_id=71a755fa-742d-4424-8523-5c53953cb5f6&ContentType_id=77eb43da-aa94-497d-a73f-5c951ff72372&Group_id=4b968841-f3e8-49da-a529-7b18e32fd69d&MonthDisplay=1&YearDisplay=2014, "Companies constantly collect personal information about their customers, like credit card information, financial account numbers and passwords. In return, I believe those companies should be responsible for securing this personal information throughout their systems that store this sensitive data," at http://www.commerce.senate.gov/public/index.cfm?p=Legislation&ContentRecord_id=40e0ad58-866a-41ea-bf00-750c17e1ee3a&ContentType_id=03ab50f5-55cd-4934-a074-d6928b9dd24c&Group_id=6eaa2a03-6e69-4e43-8597-bb12f4f5aede.

[110] In the broad term "organization," the FTC has urged the inclusion of not only private businesses but also non-profits, which it states have been subject to numerous data breaches. See Testimony of Federal Trade Commission before U.S. Congress, House of Representatives Committee on Energy and Commerce, Subcommittee on Commerce, Manufacturing, and Trade, *Protecting Consumer Information: Can Data Breaches Be Prevented?*, 113th Cong., 2nd sess., February 5, 2014, p.1, at http://docs.house.gov/meetings/IF/IF17/20140205/101714/HMTG-113-IF17-Wstate-RamirezE-20140205.pdf.

[111] Such a "reasonableness" standard was spelled out by Edith Ramirez, Chair of the FTC, in Testimony of Federal Trade Commission before U.S. Congress, House of Representatives, Committee on Energy and Commerce, Subcommittee on Commerce, Manufacturing, and Trade, *Protecting Consumer Information: Can Data Breaches Be Prevented?* 113th Cong., 2nd sess., February 5, 2014, p. 4.

[112] S. 1193, Section 2.

[113] S. 1897, Section 202.

[114] S. 1897, Section 203.

[115] S. 1927, Section 3.

[116] S. 1927, Section 5.

[117] S. 1976 is co-sponsored by Chairman of the Senate Select Intelligence Committee Senator Feinstein, Chairman of the Commerce Subcommittee on Communications, Technology, and the Internet, Senator Pryor; and Chairman of the Commerce Subcommittee on Science and Space, Senator Bill Nelson.

[118] S. 1976, Section 2.

[119] S. 1995, Section 202.

[120] S. 1995, Section 202.

[121] S. 1995, Section 202.

[122] S. 1995, Sections 203-205.

[123] Presidential Policy Directive/PPD-21, "Critical Infrastructure Security and Resilience," February 12, 2013, at http://www.whitehouse.gov/the-press-office/2013/02/12/presidential-policy-directive-critical-infrastructure-security-and-resil.

[124] Testimony of John J. Mulligan, executive vice president and chief financial officer, Target, before U.S. Congress, Senate, Committee on Commerce, Science, and Transportation, *Protecting Personal Consumer Information from Cyber Attacks and Data Breaches*, 113th Cong., 2nd sess., March 26, 2014, pp. 4-5, at http://www.commerce.senate.gov/public/?a=Files.Serve&File_id=c2103bd3-8c40-42c3-973b-bd08c7de45ef.

[125] Andrew Nolan, "National Institute of Standards and Technology Issues Long-awaited Cybersecurity Framework," CRS Legal Sidebar, March 5, 2014, at http://www.crs.gov/LegalSidebar/details.aspx?ID=829&Source=search.

[126] Ibid.

[127] Ibid.

[128] For more on this, see Richard A. Epstein and Thomas P. Brown "Cybersecurity in the Payment Card Industry," *University of Chicago Law Review*, vol. 75, no. 1 (winter, 2008), pp. 203-223, at http://www.jstor.org/stable/20141905.

[129] Richard A. Epstein and Thomas P. Brown "Cybersecurity in the Payment Card Industry," *University of Chicago Law Review*, vol. 75, no. 1 (winter, 2008), pp. 203-223 at 207.

[130] Craig Newman and Daniel Stein, "Who Should Pay for Data Theft?" *Bloomberg BusinessWeek*, February 20, 2014, at http://www.businessweek.com/articles/2014-02-20/who-should-pay-for-data-theft. See also Marcy Gordon, "Target Breach Pits Banks against Retailers," *Associated Press*, February 4, 2014, at http://bigstory.ap.org/article/target-data-breach-pits-banks-against-retailers.

[131] Epstein and Brown argue that no such legislative solution exists and that private contract negotiations are a superior solution for allocating such shared costs, but concede that proper allocation is problematic.

[132] Doug Kantor, Counsel for the Merchants Payments Coalition, "Broken Payment System Guarantees another Breach like Target's," *American Banker*, January 9, 2014, at http://www.americanbanker.com/bankthink/broken-payment-system-guarantees-another-breach-like-target-1064784-1.html.

[133] Camden Fine, President and CEO of the Independent Community Bankers of America, and Richard Hunt, President and CEO of the Consumer Bankers Association, "Banks Pay Price for Retailers' Data Breaches," *The Hill*, February 11, 2014, at http://thehill.com/blogs/congress-blog/technology/197978-banks-pay-price-for-retailers-data-breaches.

[134] Julia S. Cheney, Robert M. Hunt, Katy R. Jacob, Richard D. Porter, and Bruce J. Summers, *The Efficiency and Integrity of Payment Card Systems: Industry Views on the Risks Posed by Data Breaches*, Federal Reserve Bank of Philadelphia, Payment Cards Center Discussion Paper, October 2012, at http://www.phil.frb.org/consumer-credit-and-payments/payment-cards-center/publications/discussion-papers/2012/D-2012-Efficiency-and-Integrity-of-Payment-Card-Systems.pdf.

[135] Ibid.

[136] Ibid., p. 26.

[137] Ibid., p. 30.

[138] For example, U.S. Congress, Senate, Committee on Banking, Housing, and Urban Affairs, Subcommittee on National Security and International Trade and Finance, *Safeguarding Consumers' Financial Data*, 113th Cong., 2nd sess., comments of Senator Warner, Senator Kirk, Senator Warren, Senator Tester, Senator Menendez; and in the Senate Judiciary Committee, comments of Senator Hatch, Senator Durbin, and others. The same question was asked by Members in the other congressional committee hearings.

[139] U.S. Congress, Senate, Committee on Banking, Housing, and Urban Affairs, Subcommittee on National Security and International Trade and Finance, *Safeguarding Consumers' Financial Data*, 113th Cong., 2nd sess., comment of Senator Warren: "We understand why Chip and PIN works better. And it seems that we are years behind Europe in developing adequate technology. Technology we know is out there, but applying adequate technology here in the United States. So I was interested, in your testimony, Mr. Leach, you said that you think that standards are best left to private organizations such as yours. That's what we've done, and now we're now way behind in technology and have become the targets for data attacks from around the world.... So why should we leave this to organizations like yours? It sounds like to me we may need some pressure from the government to make sure that the toughest standards are used." at http://www.cq.com/doc/congressionaltranscripts-4417795.

[140] U.S. Congress, Senate, Committee on the Judiciary, *Privacy in the Digital Age: Preventing Data Breaches and Combating Cybercrime*, 113th Cong., 2nd sess., February 4, 2014, Comments of Senator Durbin: "Retailers and customers in many cases are paying an additional one cent on every transaction for anti-fraud measures so they are, in fact, giving the issuing banks and card companies basically a subsidy to have anti- fraud technology. So it isn't as if we aren't paying already to move this technology forward," at http://www.cq.com/doc/congressionaltranscripts-4418420.

In: The Target Store Data Breaches
Editor: Marianna Hardy
ISBN: 978-1-63321-269-5

Chapter 2

A "KILL CHAIN" ANALYSIS OF THE 2013 TARGET DATA BREACH*

Senate Committee on Commerce, Science and Transportation

EXECUTIVE SUMMARY

In November and December 2013, cyber thieves executed a successful cyber attack against Target, one of the largest retail companies in the United States. The attackers surreptitiously gained access to Target's computer network, stole the financial and personal information of as many as 110 million Target customers, and then removed this sensitive information from Target's network to a server in Eastern Europe.

This report presents an explanation of how the Target breach occurred, based on media reports and expert analyses that have been published since Target publicly acknowledged this breach on December 19, 2013. Although the complete story of how this breach took place may not be known until Target completes its forensic examination of the breach, facts already available in the public record provide a great deal of useful information about the attackers' methods and Target's defenses.

---

* This is an edited, reformatted and augmented version of a Majority Staff report, dated March 26, 2014.

This report analyzes what has been reported to date about the Target data breach, using the "intrusion kill chain" framework, an analytical tool introduced by Lockheed Martin security researchers in 2011, and today widely used by information security professionals in both the public and the private sectors. This analysis suggests that Target missed a number of opportunities along the kill chain to stop the attackers and prevent the massive data breach. Key points at which Target apparently failed to detect and stop the attack include, but are not limited to, the following:

- Target gave network access to a third-party vendor, a small Pennsylvania HVAC company, which did not appear to follow broadly accepted information security practices. The vendor's weak security allowed the attackers to gain a foothold in Target's network.
- Target appears to have failed to respond to multiple automated warnings from the company's anti-intrusion software that the attackers were installing malware on Target's system.
- Attackers who infiltrated Target's network with a vendor credential appear to have successfully moved from less sensitive areas of Target's network to areas storing consumer data, suggesting that Target failed to properly isolate its most sensitive network assets.
- Target appears to have failed to respond to multiple warnings from the company's anti-intrusion software regarding the escape routes the attackers planned to use to exfiltrate data from Target's network.

A. The Target Data Breach

1. The Stolen Data

On December 19, 2013, Target publicly confirmed that some 40 million credit and debit card accounts were exposed in a breach of its network.[1] The Target press release was published after the breach was first reported on December 18 by Brian Krebs, an independent Internet security news and investigative reporter.[2] Target officials have testified before Congress that they were not aware of the breach until contacted by the Department of Justice on December 12.[3] The data breach affected cards used in U.S. Target stores between November 27 and December 18, 2013.[4]

Source: Krebsonsecurity.com.

Figure 1. Advertisement for Stolen Target Cards.

Thieves were able to sell information from these cards via online black market forums known as “card shops.”[5] These websites list card information including the card type, expiration date, track data (account information stored on a card’s magnetic stripe), country of origin, issuing bank, and successful use rate for card batches over time. The newer the batch, the higher the price, as issuing banks often have not had sufficient time to identify and cancel compromised cards. A seller, nicknamed “Rescator,” at a notorious card shop even offered a money-back guarantee for immediately cancelled cards.[6] Those purchasing the information can then create and use counterfeit cards with the track data and PIN numbers[7] stolen from credit and debit card magnetic stripes. Fraudsters often use these cards to purchase high-dollar items and fence them for cash, and if PIN numbers are available, a thief can extract a victim’s money directly from an ATM. Based on a reading of underground forums, hackers may be attempting to decrypt the stolen Target PIN numbers.[8]

On January 10, 2014, Target disclosed that non-financial personal information, including names, addresses, phone numbers, and email addresses, for up to 70 million customers was also stolen during the data breach.[9]

2. The Attack

On January 12, Target CEO Gregg Steinhafel confirmed that malware installed on point of sale (POS) terminals[10] at U.S.-based Target stores enabled the theft of financial information from 40 million credit and debit cards.[11] This malware utilized a so-called “RAM scraping” attack, which allowed for the collection of unencrypted, plaintext data as it passed through the infected POS machine's memory before transfer to the company's payment processing provider. According to reports by Brian Krebs, a tailored version of the "BlackPOS" malware – available on black market cyber crime forums for between $1,800 and $2,300 – was installed on Target's POS machines.[12] This malware has been described by McAfee Director of Threat Intelligence Operations as "absolutely unsophisticated and uninteresting."[13] This assessment is in contrast with the statement of Lawrence Zelvin, Director of the Department of Homeland Security's National Cybersecurity and Communications Integration Center, who describes the malware used in the attack as "incredibly sophisticated."[14]

According to unnamed investigators, the attackers first installed their malware on a small number of POS terminals between November 15 and November 28, with the majority of Target's POS system infected by November 30.[15] A report by *The New York Times* states that the attackers first gained access to Target's internal network on November 12.[16]

A Dell SecureWorks report shows that the attackers also installed malware, designed to move stolen data through Target's network and the company's firewall, on a Target server.[17] The Dell SecureWorks team was able to analyze a sample of the actual malware used in the Target attack. The attackers reportedly first installed three variants of this malware on November 30 and updated it twice more, just before midnight on December 2 and just after midnight on December 3.[18] According to a *Bloomberg Businessweek* report, Target's FireEye malware intrusion detection system triggered urgent alerts with each installation of the data exfiltration malware.[19] However, Target's security team neither reacted to the alarms nor allowed the FireEye software to automatically delete the malware in question. Target's Symantec antivirus software also detected malicious behavior around November 28, implicating the same server flagged by FireEye's software.[20]

According to Seculert, a security company focused on advanced cyber threats, the malware started to send the stolen data to an external file transfer protocol (FTP) server via another compromised Target server on December 2, 2013.[21] Over the next two weeks, the attackers collected 11 GB of stolen information using a Russia-based server.[22] Analysis of the malware by Dell SecureWorks found that the attackers exfiltrated data between 10:00 a.m. and 6:00 p.m. Central Standard Time, presumably to obscure their work during Target's busier shopping hours.[23] Other sources describe a variety of external data drop locations, including compromised servers in Miami and Brazil.[24] The 70 million records of non-financial data were included in this theft, but public reports do not make clear how the attackers accessed this separate data set.

The attackers reportedly first gained access to Target's system by stealing credentials from an HVAC and refrigeration company, Fazio Mechanical Services, based in Sharpsburg, Pennsylvania.[25] This company specializes as a refrigeration contractor for supermarkets in the mid-Atlantic region[26] and had remote access to Target's network for electronic billing, contract submission, and project management purposes.[27]

Reports indicate that at least two months before the Target data breach began, attackers stole Fazio Mechanical's credentials for accessing Target's network via emails infected with malware.[28] According to a former Target security team member, Fazio would more than likely have had access to Target's Ariba external billing system;[29] however, reports do not make clear how the attackers gained access to Target's POS terminals from this initial foothold on the edge of Target's network. According to the same source, it is likely the outside portal was not fully isolated from the rest of Target's network.[30] Once inside, the attackers may have exploited a default account name used by an IT management software product by BMC Software to move within Target's network.[31] The attackers also disguised their data exfiltration malware as a legitimate BMC Software product.[32]

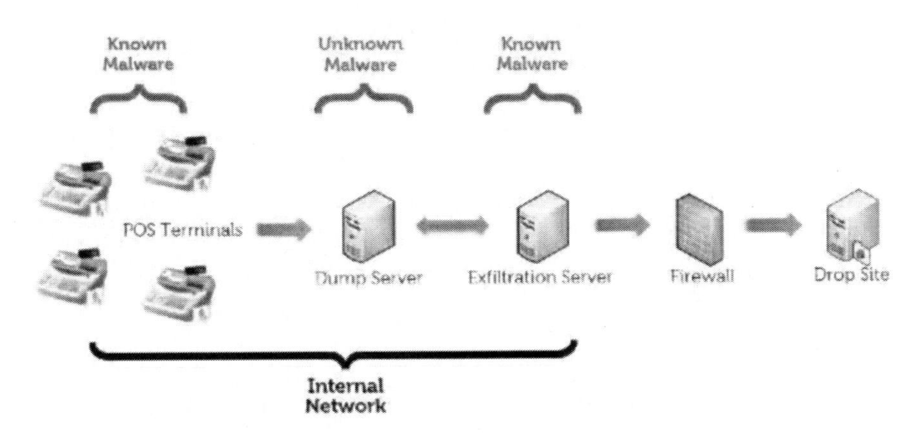

Source: Dell SecureWorks.

Figure 2. Diagram of Data Exfiltration.

B. THE KILL CHAIN

1. The "Kill Chain" As a Cybersecurity Defense Tool

The conventional model of information security relies on static defense (e.g. intrusion detection systems and antivirus software) and assumes that attackers have an inherent advantage over defenders given ever-shifting technologies and undiscovered software vulnerabilities. In 2011, the Lockheed Martin Computer Incident Response Team staff published a white paper explaining how these conventional defenses were not sufficient to protect organizations from sophisticated "advanced persistent threats" (APTs).[33] The paper proposed an "intelligence-driven, threat-focused approach to study intrusions from the adversaries' perspective" that could give network defenders the upper hand in fighting cyber attackers.[34]

Instead of installing static defense tools and waiting for the next attack, the paper argued, network defenders should continuously monitor their systems for evidence that attackers are trying to gain access to their systems. Any intrusion attempt reveals important information about an attacker's tactics and methodology. Defenders can use the intelligence they gather about an attacker's playbook to "anticipate and mitigate future intrusions based on knowledge of the threat."[35] When a defender analyzes the actions of attackers, finds patterns, and musters resources to address capability gaps, "it raises the costs an adversary must expend to achieve their objectives ... [and] such aggressors have no inherent advantage over defenders."[36]

To illustrate how network defenders can act on their knowledge of their adversaries' tactics, the paper lays out the multiple steps an attacker must proceed through to plan and execute an attack. These steps are the "kill chain." While the attacker must complete all of these steps to execute a successful attack, the defender only has to stop the attacker from completing any one of these steps to thwart the attack.

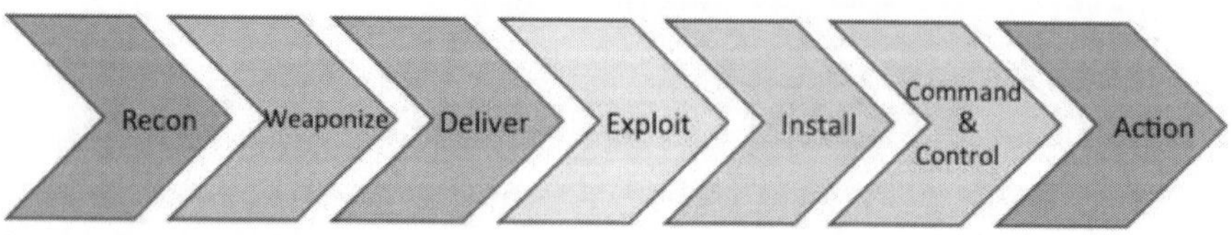

Source: Lockheed Martin.

Figure 3. Diagram of the Intrusion Kill Chain.

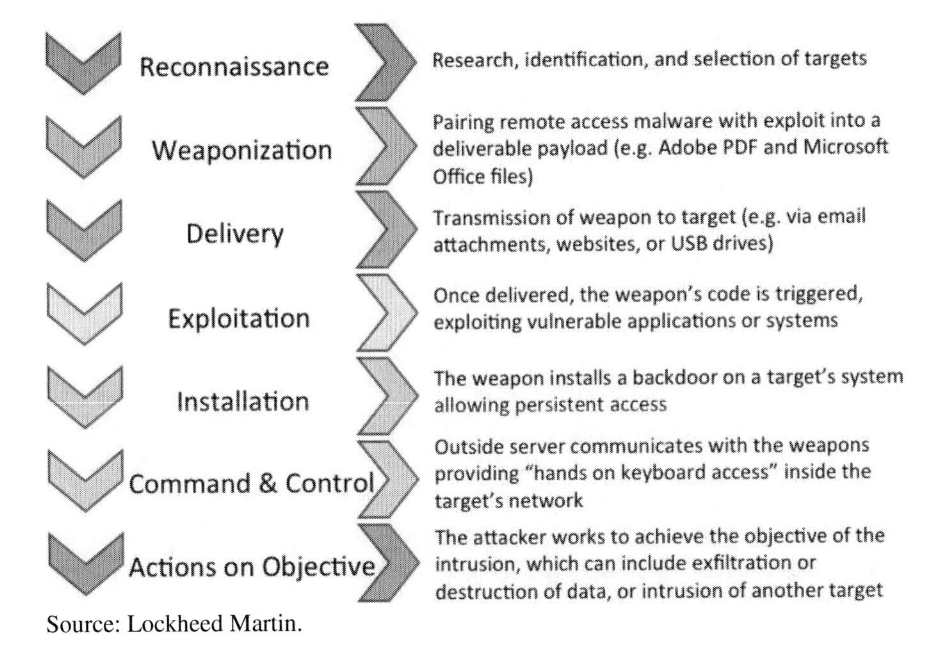

Source: Lockheed Martin.

Figure 4. Phases of the Intrusion Kill Chain.

Analyzing past attacks, utilizing threat intelligence, and improving defenses at all phases of the kill chain allow a defender to detect and deny future attacks earlier and earlier in the kill chain. This requires constant vigilance, but it can theoretically defend against even APTs using so-called "zero-day" exploits, which utilize previously unknown vulnerabilities and attack signatures that defense tools cannot detect.[37]

2. Analysis of the Target Data Breach Using the Kill Chain

John Mulligan, Target's Executive Vice President and Chief Financial Officer, testified that his company "had in place multiple layers of protection, including firewalls, malware detection software, intrusion detection and prevention capabilities and data loss prevention tools."[38] He further stated that Target had been certified in September 2013 as compliant with the Payment Card Industry Data Security Standards (PCI-DSS),[39] which credit card companies require before allowing merchants to process credit and debit card payments.

These steps were obviously not sufficient to prevent the breach. Based on public information about Target's breach reviewed in the previous section, this section walks through the steps of the kill chain and analyzes what actions Target and its contractor, Fazio Mechanical Services, did or did not take to defend themselves.

A. Reconnaissance – Attacker Quietly Gathers Information about Victim

As discussed above, the attacker may have sent malware-laden emails to Fazio at least two months before the Target data breach began. According to analysis by Brian Krebs, the attacker may have found information on Target's third-party vendors through simple Internet searches, which, at the time of his writing, displayed Target's supplier portal and facilities management pages.[40] Files available on these sites provided information for HVAC vendors and, through a metadata analysis, allowed the attacker to map Target's internal network prior to the breach. To disrupt this step in the kill chain, Target could have limited the amount of publicly available vendor information. Target could have also shared threat information with its suppliers and vendors and encouraged collaboration on security within the community.

B. Weaponization – Attacker Prepares Attack Payload to Deliver to Victim

While unconfirmed, the attacker likely weaponized its malware targeting Fazio in an email attachment, likely a PDF or Microsoft Office document. Fazio could have disrupted this step in the kill chain through the use of broadly accepted real-time monitoring and anti-malware software. However, according to investigators familiar with the case, Fazio used the free version of Malwarebytes Anti-Malware, which does not provide real-time protection and is intended only for individual consumer use.[41]

C. Delivery – Attacker Sends Payload to Victim

The attacker sent infected emails to Fazio in a so-called phishing attack. Phishing, or "spear phishing," when an attacker customizes email messages using social engineering techniques (e.g. checking Facebook or LinkedIn for a potential victim's business associates and relationships), is a well-known attack method. Fazio could have disrupted this step in the kill chain by training its staff to recognize and report phishing emails. Real-time monitoring and anti-malware software could have also potentially detected the infected file(s).

While reports are unconfirmed, the malware on Fazio's systems may have recorded passwords and provided the attackers with their key to Target's Ariba external billing system. In this phase of the kill chain, Target could have potentially disrupted the attack by requiring two- factor authentication for its vendors. Two-factor authentication includes a regular password system augmented by a second step, such as providing a code sent to the vendor's mobile phone or answering extra security questions. According to a former Target vendor manager, Target rarely required two-factor authentication from its low-level contractors.[42] PCI-DSS require two- factor authentication for remote access to payment networks and access controls for all users,[43] although the Ariba system is not technically related to Target's POS system.

However the attackers actually leveraged their access to this vendor's system to enter Target's network, less security at the perimeter of Target's network may have contributed to the attackers' success in breaching the most sensitive area of Target's network containing cardholder data. Using the Fazio credentials to gain access to Target's inner network, it appears the attackers then directly uploaded their RAM scraping malware to POS terminals.

D. Exploitation – Attackers Payload Deployed in Victim's Network

Once delivered, the RAM scraping malware and exfiltration malware began recording millions of card swipes and storing the stolen data for later exfiltration. Target could have potentially blocked the effect of the exfiltration malware on its servers by either allowing its FireEye software to delete any detected malware, or, if not choosing the automatic option, by following up on the several alerts that were triggered at the time of malware delivery. According to *Businessweek*, the FireEye software sent an alert with the generic name "malware.binary" to Target security staff.[44] It is possible that Target staff could have viewed this alert as a false positive if the system was frequently alarming.

Another protective step could have been paying greater attention to industry and government intelligence analyses. According to an FBI industry notification, RAM scraping malware has been observed since 2011.[45] Furthermore, a *Reuters* report stated that Visa published in April and August of 2013 two warnings about the use of RAM scraping malware in attacks targeting retailers.[46] These warnings apparently included recommendations for reducing the risk of a successful attack. According to the *Wall Street Journal*, Target's security staff made their misgivings known about vulnerabilities on the company's POS system; however, it is unclear if Target took any action to address vulnerabilities before the attack.[47]

E. Installation – Attacker Establishes Foothold in Victim's Network

Reports suggest that the attacker maintained access to Fazio's systems for some time while attempting to further breach Target's network. It is unclear exactly how the attacker could have escalated its access from the Ariba external billing system to deeper layers of Target's internal network. But given the installation of the BlackPOS malware on Target's POS terminals, the compromise of 70 million records of non-financial data, and the compromise of the internal Target servers used to gather stolen data, it appears that the attackers succeeded in moving through various key Target systems.

Brian Krebs and Dell SecureWorks posit that the attackers may have exploited a default account name used in a BMC Software information technology management system;[48] however, it is unclear exactly how the attackers found the account password. If the theory is true, a protective step at this phase of the kill chain could have included the elimination or alteration of unneeded default accounts, as called for in PCI-DSS 2.1.[49]

In its recently filed 10K, Target states that in the fall of 2013, "an independent third-party assessor found the portion of our network that handles payment card information to be compliant with applicable data security standards."[50] One of those standards would have been PCI-DSS 11.5, which requires vendors to monitor the integrity of critical system files.[51] To achieve this standard, Target could have used a technique called "white listing," whereby only approved processes are allowed to run on a machine.

F. Command and Control (C2) – Attacker Has "Hands on the Keyboard" Remote Access to Victim's Network

Based on the reported timeline of the breach, the attackers had access to Target's internal network for over a month and compromised internal servers with exfiltration malware by November 30. While the exact method by which the attackers maintained command and control is unknown, it is clear the attackers were able to maintain a line of communication between the outside Internet and Target's cardholder network.

In this phase of the kill chain, one protective step includes analysis of the location of credentialed users in the network. For example, if the attackers were still using Fazio's stolen credentials, an analyst would have reason to be concerned if that credential was being used in an unrelated area of the Target network. That the attackers were still using Fazio's credentials when installing malware or moving through the Target network is unlikely, but the analysis could have still proven useful.

Another protective step at this phase would have been strong firewalls between Target's internal systems and the outside Internet (e.g., routing traffic through a proxy) to help disrupt the attacker's command and control. Target could also have filtered or blocked certain Internet connections commonly used for command and control.

G. Actions on Objectives – Attacker Acts to Accomplish Data Exfiltration

The attackers transmitted the stolen data to outside servers – at least one of which was located in Russia – in plain text via FTP[52] (a standard method for transferring files) over the course of two weeks. At this phase of the kill chain, protective defensive steps could have included white listing approved FTP servers to which Target's network is allowed to upload data. For example, a white list could have dismissed connections between Target's network and Russia-based Internet servers. An analysis of data transmissions on Target's busy network may be like searching for a needle in a haystack, but an upload to a server in Russia presumably would have been flagged as suspicious if discovered.

Target's FireEye software reportedly did detect the data exfiltration malware and decoded the destination of servers on which data for millions of stolen credit cards were stored for days at a time. Acting on this information could have stopped the exfiltration, not only at this last stage, but especially during the "delivery" step on the kill chain.

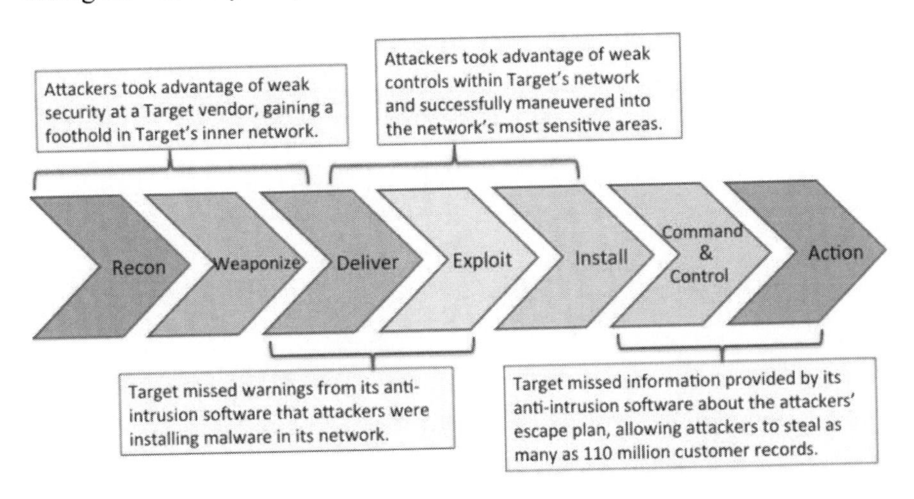

Figure 5. Target's Possible Missed Opportunities.

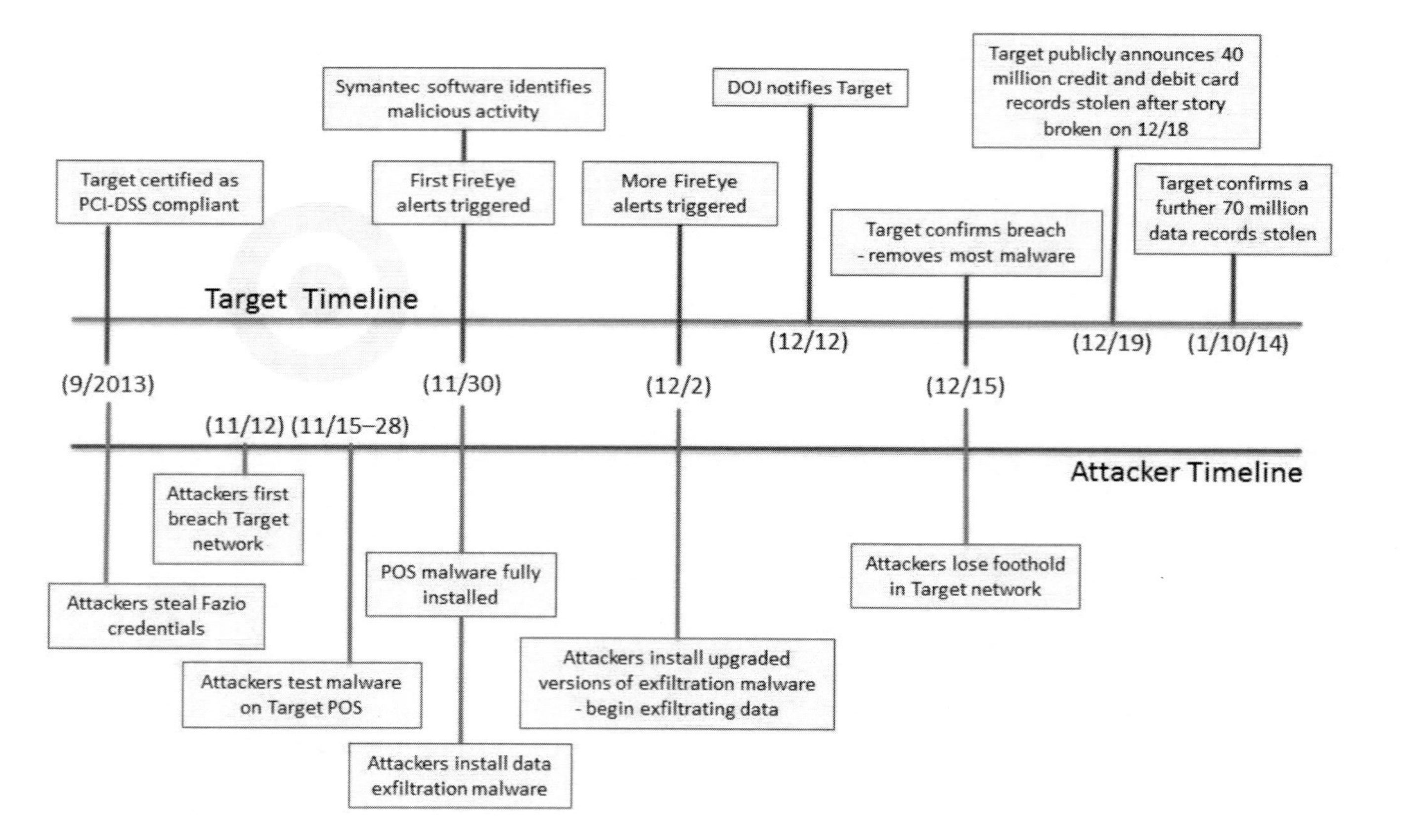

Figure 6. A Timeline of the Target Data Breach.

APPENDIX I.

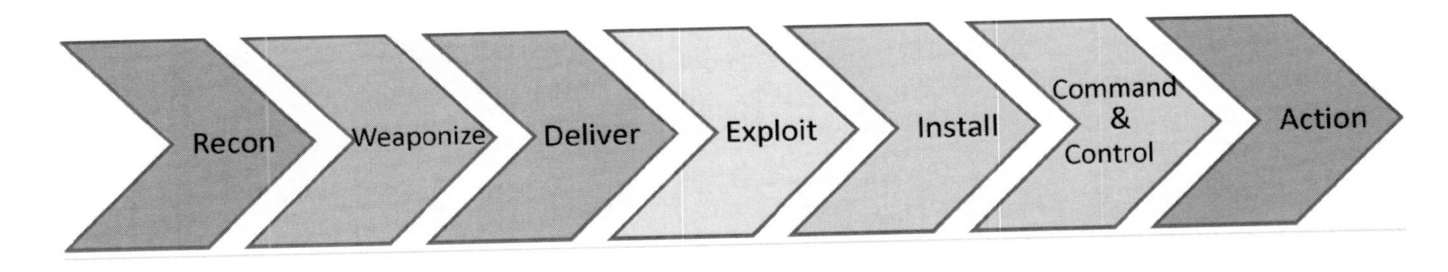

The Intrusion Kill Chain.

APPENDIX II.

Phases of the Intrusion Kill Chain.

APPENDIX III.

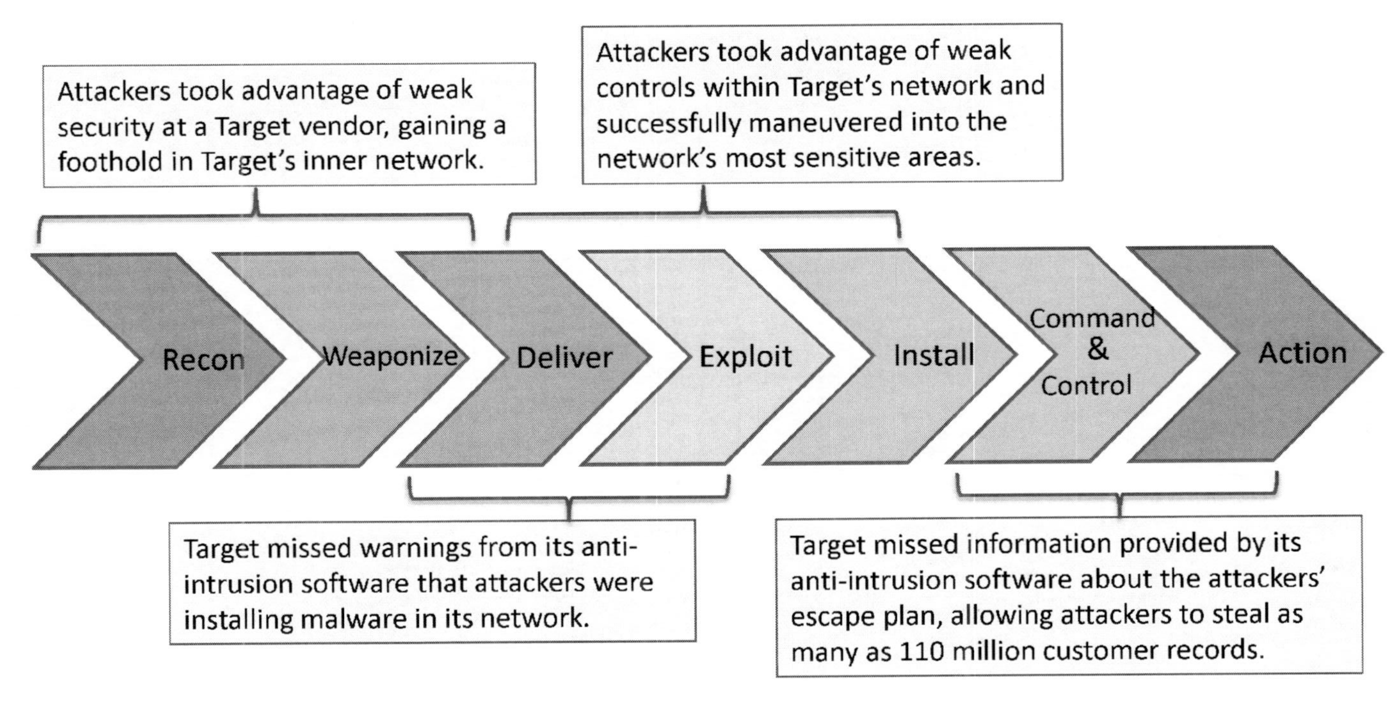

Target's Possible Missed Opportunities.

APPENDIX IV.

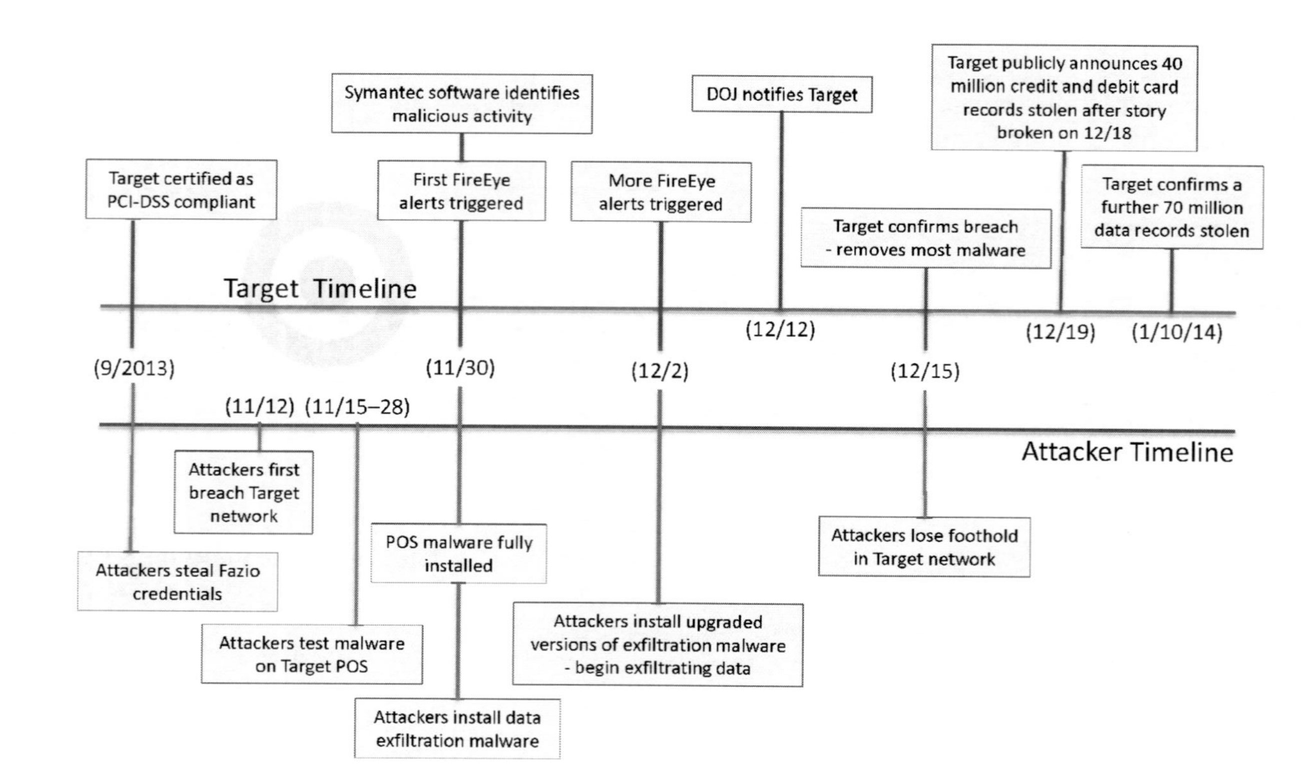

A Timeline of the Target Data Breach.

End Notes

[1] Target, *Target Confirms Unauthorized Access to Payment Card Data in U.S. Stores* (Dec. 19, 2013) (online at http://pressroom.target.com/news/target-confirms-unauthorized-access-to-payment-card-data- in-u-s-stores).

[2] Brian Krebs, *Sources: Target Investigating Data Breach*, KrebsOnSecurity (Dec. 18, 2013) (online at http://krebsonsecurity.com/2013/12/sources-target-investigating-data-breach/).

[3] Testimony of John Mulligan, Target Executive Vice President and Chief Financial Officer, before the Senate Committee on the Judiciary, at 2 (Feb. 4, 2014) (online at http://www.judiciary.senate.gov/pdf/02-04-14MulliganTestimony.pdf).

[4] *Id.* at 2-3.

[5] Brian Krebs, *Cards Stolen in Target Breach Flood Underground Markets* (Dec. 20, 2013) (online at http://krebsonsecurity.com/2013/12/cards-stolen-in-target-breach-flood-underground-markets/).

[6] *Id.*

[7] Target initially denied that debit card PIN numbers had been stolen, but reports confirmed that encrypted PIN numbers had indeed been stolen. *See* Jim Finkle and David Henry, *Exclusive: Target Hackers Stole Encrypted Bank PINs – Source*, Reuters (Dec. 25, 2013) (online at http://www.reuters.com/article/2013/12/25/us-target-databreach-idUSBRE9BN0L 220131225).

[8] Adam Greenberg, *Hackers Seek to Decrypt PIN Codes Likely Stolen in Target Breach*, SC Magazine (Jan. 8, 2014) (online at http://www.scmagazine.com/hackers-seek-to-decrypt-pin-codes-likely-stolen-in- target-breach/article/328529/).

[9] Target, *Target Provides Update on Data Breach and Financial Performance* (Jan. 10, 2014) (online at http://pressroom.target.com/news/target-provides-update-on-data-breach-and-financial-performance).

[10] A Point of Sale (POS) terminal is a physical device used by a merchant to process payments for goods and services purchased by a customer. Customized hardware and software is often used at a POS terminal, or cash register, part of which is used to swipe and process credit and debit card information.

[11] Becky Quick, *Target CEO Defends 4-Day Wait to Disclose Massive Data Hack*, CNBC (Jan. 12, 2014) (online at http://www.cnbc.com/id/101329300).

[12] Brian Krebs, *A First Look at the Target Intrusion, Malware*, KrebsOnSecurity (Jan. 15, 2014) (online at http://krebsonsecurity.com/2014/01/a-first-look-at-the-target-intrusion-malware/).

[13] Michael Riley, Ben Elgin, Dune Lawrence, and Carol Matlack, *Missed Alarms and 40 Million Stolen Credit Card Numbers: How Target Blew It*, Bloomberg Businessweek (Mar. 13, 2014) (online at http://www.businessweek.com/articles/2014-03-13/target-missed-alarms-in-epic-hack-of-credit-card- data).

[14] House Committee on Energy and Commerce, Subcommittee on Commerce, Manufacturing, and Trade, *Protecting Consumer Information: Can Data Breaches Be Prevented?*, 113th Cong. (Feb. 5, 2014).

[15] Brian Krebs, *Target Hackers Broke in Via HVAC Company*, KrebsOnSecurity (Feb. 5, 2014) (online at http://krebsonsecurity.com/2014/02/target-hackers-broke-in-via-hvac-company/).

[16] Elizabeth A. Harris, Nicole Perlroth, Nathaniel Popper, and Hilary Stout, *A Sneaky Path Into Target Customers' Wallets* (Jan. 17, 2014) (online at http://www.nytimes.com/2014/01/18/business/a-sneaky-path-into-target-customers-wallets.html).

[17] A third type of malware was installed on intermediate servers which presumably stored stolen data inside Target's network before the next exfiltration step. However, this malware has thus far not been analyzed publicly. *See* Keith Jarvis and Jason Milletary, *Inside a Targeted Point-of-Sale Data Breach*, Dell SecureWorks, at 5 (Jan. 24, 2014) (online at http://krebsonsecurity.com/wp-content/uploads/2014/01/Inside-a-Targeted-Point-of-Sale-Data-Breach.pdf).

[18] *Id.*

[19] Michael Riley, Ben Elgin, Dune Lawrence, and Carol Matlack, *Missed Alarms and 40 Million Stolen Credit Card Numbers: How Target Blew It*, Bloomberg Businessweek (Mar. 13, 2014) (online at http://www.businessweek.com/articles/2014-03-13/target-missed-alarms-in-epic-hack-of-credit-card- data).

[20] *Id.*

[21] Aviv Raff, *PoS Malware Targeted Target*, Seculert (Jan. 16, 2014) (online at http://www.seculert.com/blog/2014/01/pos-malware-targeted-target.html).

[22] *Id.*

[23] Keith Jarvis and Jason Milletary, *Inside a Targeted Point-of-Sale Data Breach*, Dell SecureWorks, at 6, 11 (Jan. 24, 2014) (online at http://krebsonsecurity.com/wp-content/uploads/2014/01/Inside-a-Targeted- Point-of-Sale-Data-Breach.pdf).

[24] Brian Krebs, *Target Hackers Broke in Via HVAC Company*, KrebsOnSecurity (Feb. 5, 2014) (online at http://krebsonsecurity.com/2014/02/target-hackers-broke-in-via-hvac-company/).

[25] *Id.*

[26] Fazio Mechanical Services, *About Us* (accessed Mar. 12, 2014) (online at http://faziomechanical.com/about-us.html).

[27] Fazio Mechanical Services, *Statement on Target Data Breach* (accessed Mar. 12, 2014) (online at http://faziomechanical.com/Target-Breach-Statement.pdf).

[28] Sources have identified malware known as "Citadel," which steals passwords on compromised machines. However, this has not been confirmed. *See* Brian Krebs, *Email Attack on Vendor Set Up Breach at Target*, KrebsOnSecurity (Feb. 12, 2014) (online at http://krebsonsecurity.com/2014/02/email- attack-on-vendor-set-up-breach-at-target/).

[29] *Id.*

[30] *Id.*

[31] Brian Krebs, *New Clues in the Target Breach*, KrebsOnSecurity (Jan. 29, 2014) (online at http://krebsonsecurity.com/2014/01/new-clues-in-the-target-breach/).

[32] Keith Jarvis and Jason Milletary, *Inside a Targeted Point-of-Sale Data Breach*, Dell SecureWorks, at 6 (Jan. 24, 2014) (online at http://krebsonsecurity.com/wp-content/uploads/2014/01/Inside-a-Targeted- Point-of-Sale-Data-Breach.pdf).

[33] Eric M. Hutchins, Michael J. Cloppert, Rohan M. Amin, *Intelligence-Driven Computer Network Defense Informed by Analysis of Adversary Campaigns and Intrusion Kill Chains*, Lockheed Martin (2011) (online at http://www.lockheedmartin.com/content/dam/lockheed/data/corporate/documents/LM- White-Paper-Intel-Driven-Defense.pdf).

[34] *Id.* at 2.

[35] *Id.*

[36] *Id.* at 3.

[37] *Id.* at 4-5.

[38] Testimony of John Mulligan, Target Executive Vice President and Chief Financial Officer, before the Senate Committee on the Judiciary, at 4-5 (Feb. 4, 2014) (online at http://www.judiciary.senate.gov/pdf/02-04-14MulliganTestimony.pdf).

[39] *Id.* at 5.

[40] Brian Krebs, *Email Attack on Vendor Set Up Breach at Target*, KrebsOnSecurity (Feb. 12, 2014) (online at http://krebsonsecurity.com/2014/02/email-attack-on-vendor-set-up-breach-at-target/).

[41] *Id.*

[42] *Id.*

[43] Standard 7.2 and 8.3 are most relevant to this discussion. Version 3.0 of the standard was released in November 2013, after the Target breach. As such, this report references the previous version 2.0. *See* Payment Card Industry Security Standards Council, *Payment Card Industry (PCI) Data Security Standard Version 2.0*, at 44, 47 (Oct. 2010) (online at https://www.pcisecuritystandards.org/documents/pci_dss_v2.pdf).

[44] Michael Riley, Ben Elgin, Dune Lawrence, and Carol Matlack, *Missed Alarms and 40 Million Stolen Credit Card Numbers: How Target Blew It*, Bloomberg Businessweek (Mar. 13, 2014) (online at http://www.businessweek.com/articles/2014-03-13/target-missed-alarms-in-epic-hack-of-credit-card- data).

[45] FBI Cyber Division, *Recent Cyber Intrusion Events Directed Toward Retail Firms* (Jan. 17, 2014) (online at http://krebsonsecurity.com/wp-content/uploads/2014/01/FBI-CYD-PIN-140117-001.pdf).

[46] Jim Finkle and Mark Hosenball, *Exclusive: More Well-Known U.S. Retailers Victims of Cyber Attacks – Sources*, Reuters (Jan 12, 2014) (online at http://www.reuters.com/article/2014/01/12/us-target-databreach-retailers-idUSBREA0B01720140112).

[47] Danny Yadron, Paul Ziobro, Devlin Barrett, *Target Warned of Vulnerabilities Before Data Breach*, The Wall Street Journal (Feb. 14, 2014) (online at http://online.wsj.com/news/articles/SB10001424052702304703804579381520736715690).

[48] Brian Krebs, *New Clues in the Target Breach*, KrebsOnSecurity (Jan. 29, 2014) (online at http://krebsonsecurity.com/2014/01/new-clues-in-the-target-breach/); Keith Jarvis and Jason Milletary, *Inside a Targeted Point-of-Sale Data Breach*, Dell SecureWorks, at 5 (Jan. 24, 2014) (online at http://krebsonsecurity.com/wp-content/uploads/2014/01/Inside-a-Targeted-Point-of-Sale-Data- Breach.pdf).

[49] Payment Card Industry Security Standards Council, *Payment Card Industry (PCI) Data Security Standard Version 2.0*, at 24 (Oct. 2010) (online at https://www.pcisecurity standards.org/documents/pci_dss_v2.pdf).

[50] Target Corporation, SEC Form 10-K, at 17, 47 (Mar. 14, 2014) (online at http://www.sec.gov/Archives/edgar/data/27419/000002741914000014/tgt-20140201x10k.htm).

[51] Payment Card Industry Security Standards Council, *Payment Card Industry (PCI) Data Security Standard Version 2.0*, at 63 (Oct. 2010) (online at https://www.pcisecurity standards.org/documents/pci_dss_v2.pdf).

[52] McAfee, *McAfee Labs Threats Report Fourth Quarter 2013*, at 7 (2013) (online at http://www.mcafee.com/us/resources/reports/rp-quarterly-threat-q4-2013.pdf).

In: The Target Store Data Breaches
Editor: Marianna Hardy
ISBN: 978-1-63321-269-5

Chapter 3

STATEMENT OF SENATOR PATRICK LEAHY, CHAIRMAN, SENATE JUDICIARY COMMITTEE. HEARING ON "PRIVACY IN THE DIGITAL AGE: PREVENTING DATA BREACHES AND COMBATING CYBERCRIME"*

Today, the Judiciary Committee meets to examine how we can protect Americans from the growing dangers of data breaches and cybercrime in the digital age. Safeguarding American consumers and businesses from data breaches and cybercrime has been a priority of this Committee since 2005. For years, I have worked closely with Members on both sides of the aisle to advance meaningful data privacy legislation. I thank Senator Grassley for working closely with me on this hearing. I hope we can continue working together to advance the Personal Data Privacy and Security Act that I recently reintroduced to protect American consumers.

Like many Americans, I am alarmed by the recent data breaches at Target, Neiman Marcus, and Michaels Stores. The investigations into those cyberattacks are ongoing. Yet, it is already clear that these attacks have compromised the privacy and security of millions of American consumers — potentially putting one in three Americans at risk of identity theft and other cybercrimes.

* This is an edited, reformatted and augmented version of an opening statement presented February 4, 2014 at a hearing of the Senate Judiciary Committee.

Public confidence is crucial to our economy. If consumers lose faith in business' ability to protect their personal information, our economic recovery will falter. Unfortunately, in the digital age, major data breaches involving our private information are not uncommon. The threat and dangers of data breaches are also not unique to the retail industry. There have been significant data breaches involving Sony, Epsilon, and Coca-Cola, as well as Federal government agencies, such as the Departments of Veterans Affairs and Energy. In the past few days, we have also learned of data breaches at Yahoo! and White Lodging, the hotel management company for national hotel chains such as Marriott and Starwood.

According to the Privacy Rights Clearinghouse, more than 662 million records have been involved in data breaches since 2005. A 2013 Verizon report also found that there were more than 600 publicly disclosed data breaches just last year.

No one would dispute that businesses need to thoroughly assess the damage when a cyberattack is discovered. But time is of the essence for law enforcement seeking to catch the perpetrators, and also for consumers who want to protect themselves against further exposure. American consumers deserve to know when their private information has been compromised and what a business is doing in response to a cyberattack.

We should remember that the businesses that suffer cyberattacks are also often the victims of a cybercrime. A recent study sponsored by Symantec found that data breaches involving malicious cyberattacks are the most costly data breaches around the globe. The per capita cost of such cyberattacks in the United States was $277 per compromised record in 2013 — the highest cost for any nation surveyed, according to the report. This high cost is especially alarming in the midst of the fragile economic recovery.

Before the Judiciary Committee today are representatives of Target and Neiman Marcus, as well as Consumers Union and Symantec. Later, we will also hear from the United States Secret Service, the Department of Justice, and the Federal Trade Commission, who are here to provide insight into how our government is protecting American consumers and businesses from the growing threats of data breaches and cybercrime.

In the digital age, Americans face threats to their privacy and security unlike any time before in Nation's our history. I hope that all Members of the Committee will join me in responding to this urgent problem by supporting my data privacy legislation. I thank all of our witnesses for being with us today.

In: The Target Store Data Breaches
Editor: Marianna Hardy
ISBN: 978-1-63321-269-5

Chapter 4

STATEMENT OF DELARA DERAKHSHANI, POLICY COUNSEL, CONSUMERS UNION. HEARING ON "PRIVACY IN THE DIGITAL AGE: PREVENTING DATA BREACHES AND COMBATING CYBERCRIME"*

Chairman Leahy, Ranking Member Grassley, and esteemed members of the Committee. Thank you for the opportunity to testify before you today about data breaches. My name is Delara Derakhshani, and I serve as policy counsel for Consumers Union, the policy and advocacy arm of Consumer Reports.

This past December – at the height of the holiday shopping season – 40 million unsuspecting consumers learned that criminals may have gained unauthorized access to their credit and debit card numbers. Subsequently, 70 million more Target customers learned that personal information such as names, home addresses and telephone numbers may have also fallen into the hands of suspected criminal hackers. We now also know of similar breaches at other retailers: Neiman Marcus confirmed unauthorized access to payment data, and – most recently – Michael's has reported that it is investigating whether a similar breach occurred. The press is reporting that this may be the tip of the iceberg because versions of the malware that was reportedly used in

* This is an edited, reformatted and augmented version of a statement presented February 4, 2014 before a hearing of the Senate Judiciary Committee.

the Target and Neiman Marcus cyberattacks was sold to cybercriminals overseas.

This is truly disturbing. The threats from such breaches are real – and they are serious. As Consumer Reports and Consumers Union have reported with regularity in our publications, consumers who have their data compromised in a large-scale security breach are more likely to become victims of identity theft or fraud. Although federal consumer protection lending laws and voluntary industry practices generally protect consumers from significant out-of-pocket losses, consumers, policymakers, and regulators should take this threat seriously – not only to prevent fraudulent charges which in the end could wind up coming out of the pockets of the retailers, but also because a security breach exposes consumers to unpredictable risks that their personal data will be used without their authorization and for nefarious purposes.

Then there are the very practical and time-consuming concerns for consumers whose personal data has been breached. Consumers have to cancel cards, and must monitor their credit reports and continue to do so in the future. Even though millions have not yet experienced a problem, the threat and uncertainty are there. Of particular concern are debit cards which carry fewer legal protections. While consumers might not ultimately be held responsible if someone steals their debit card and pin number, data thieves can still empty out consumers' bank accounts and set off a cascade of bounced checks and late fees which victims will have to settle down the road.

Clearly, the burden is being put on consumers to be vigilant to prevent future fraudulent use of their information.

What can happen to the data after it's stolen is disconcerting, to say the least. Sometimes, data is resold to criminals outside of the country. Other times, it is used to create counterfeit credit cards or debit cards with direct access to your checking account. Even if you do not wind up becoming a victim of identity theft or have your card used for fraudulent purposes, the result is decreased consumer confidence in the marketplace and uncertainty with the realization that your private financial data is in the ether, and could one day be accessible to individuals for any purpose whatsoever.

Furthermore, in the wake of these breaches, a number of scam artists are trying to take advantage of the situation. What is happening is that scammers are trying to prey on concerns about compromised data. These scammers are attempting to gather consumers' personal and credit information – sometimes through a method called "phishing." We have urged consumers to verify the authenticity of any breach-related messages they receive, and to be wary of emails and phone calls offering identity theft or fraud protection.

When Consumers Union learned of the breach, we wrote to the CFPB, urging them to investigate the matter and for increased public disclosure. Just last week, Attorney General Eric Holder confirmed that the Department of Justice is also investigating the matter. We know lawmakers have urged the Federal Trade Commission to investigate as well. We are grateful that the federal agencies – and State Attorneys General – are on the case, so that we can get to the bottom of who did this and how it happened. And together we can formulate policies and procedures to prevent data breaches from occurring in the future.

Consumers Union and Consumer Reports have also provided consumers with a number of tips to protect themselves – such as closely monitoring their accounts, checking their financial statements frequently, and notifying their financial institutions of any suspicious card activity immediately. For extra protection, consumers can replace credit card numbers as well as debit cards and PIN numbers. We explained that consumers affected by a breach can go online and request a 90-day fraud alert on their credit reports with the three national credit bureaus – Equifax, Experian, and TransUnion – so that they can be notified if thieves try to open up a new credit account in their name. This type of new account fraud is rare and requires a Social Security number – and there's no evidence at this time that hackers have access to consumers' Social Security numbers. But consumers should know that this additional protection is available to them if they want it. Consumers may also want to place a security freeze on their credit report – which blocks access to your credit file by lenders who don't already do business with you. Finally, we have urged consumers not to waste $120 to $300 a year on so-called identity theft protection services. As we've pointed out, consumers can protect themselves for little or nothing. Some of these services use deceptive marketing to sell overpriced and useless products to consumers.

Target and affected retailers are also offering consumers credit monitoring. We believe there are some things that consumers should consider before they enroll in these services. First, consumers should recognize that these services are only free for a year. Although Target assures consumers that they will not be automatically re-enrolled, consumers may get sales solicitations when the free period ends. Second, as some consumer advocates have pointed out, in order to sign up, consumers have to agree to mandatory arbitration, which means that they waive their right to go to court should a dispute arise.

It is important to point out that we should also focus on what needs to be done to help avoid data breaches in the first place. The credit cards and debit cards most Americans use are surprisingly vulnerable to fraud, relying on decades-old technology that makes them susceptible. American credit and debit card data are usually stored unencrypted on a magnetic stripe on the back of each card. Thieves can cheaply and easily "skim" the data off of this magnetic stripe when a credit or debit card is swiped and create a counterfeit card that can access a cardholder's account at an ATM.

Many other countries have shifted or are in the process of shifting to what is known as EMV "smart cards" – or chip and pin technology, which utilizes multiple layers of security – including a computer chip in each card that stores and transmits encrypted data, as well as a unique identifier that can change with each transaction. Cardholders also enter a PIN to authorize transactions. Total fraud losses dropped by 50 percent and card counterfeiting fell by 78 percent in the first year after EMV smart cards were introduced in France in 1992. The United States has lagged behind because replacing all payment cards, updating ATMs to accept the new cards, and updating the terminals in retail stores all cost money. Some financial institutions have indicated that they will switch over to this new technology in the next few years. We need a stronger commitment from all stakeholders to adopt this technology sooner rather than later. We believe it is money well-spent, and it is a penny-wise pound-foolish philosophy to wait any longer, particularly when the burden of guarding against harm following a breach falls most squarely on the shoulders of innocent consumers whose data was compromised.

Policymakers must also take action to encourage investments in new technology to help financial institutions tighten up the own security to help prevent fraud. We need to make sure that we don't fall further behind the rest of the world in fraud protection.

These incidents reinforce just how timely and relevant this Committee's efforts are to guard against data breaches and to quickly help consumers should a breach occur. We appreciate the efforts of Chairman Leahy and the Committee on data breaches, and we recognize the long history of involvement in the topic.

The current legislation introduced by the Chairman, the Personal Data Privacy and Security Act of 2014, would encourage companies to be proactive about safeguarding the data that is entrusted to them.

We applaud the sponsors' desire to ensure that consumers are notified when a breach occurs. We believe that the sooner consumers know that their data has been compromised, the sooner they can take steps to protect themselves. We would therefore urge the Committee to consider shortening the timeline for notification from the 60 days currently in the bill to require more immediate notification. We appreciate the bill's provisions to require companies to identify security vulnerabilities, and periodically assess whether their data privacy and security programs are able to address current threats.

We are also pleased that the bill grants enforcement power to both the Federal Trade Commission and State Attorneys General. The enforcement provisions of the bill are a crucial element of a data security framework, and as we have stated previously – we strongly believe that State Attorneys General must be involved in such enforcement. State Attorneys General have been at the forefront of notice and data breach issues and have played an invaluable role in the efforts to address identity theft and data breaches.

In testimony to Congress on this matter, Consumers Union has repeatedly pointed out that the strongest state notice of breach laws do not require a finding of risk before requiring notification to consumers. Although Consumers Union would prefer that consumers receive notification anytime their personal information is compromised – if there is to be a standard for risk, then Consumers Union would prefer the approach taken by this bill – in which the risk is considered an exemption rather than an affirmative trigger. Under this exemption approach, insufficient information about the level of risk does not eliminate a company's obligation to tell consumers about the breach.

Nevertheless, we would like to strengthen some provisions in the bill, including those related to pre-emption. We want to make sure that any national standard results in strong, meaningful protections for consumers – but that any federal standard does not tie the hands of states or limit their ability to adopt additional protective measures for consumers. Our organization supported the California breach law passed in 2002 and enacted in 2003, and we have a long history of working with state legislatures to pass initiatives that would protect consumers. As a result, we would certainly urge that any federal law addressing data breach and notification set out a floor – not a ceiling – allowing states the freedom to innovate in order to address new threats to consumers.

In closing, thank you for the opportunity to speak before you today. We appreciate the Committee's interest in data security, and we encourage policymakers and regulators to continue to press for responsible data security practices with a new urgency. We all want to ensure consumer confidence in the marketplace. Data breaches undermine that confidence and place unfair burdens on consumers. We look forward to working with the Committee and other stakeholders to make sure that consumers – and their information – are protected adequately. Thank you.

In: The Target Store Data Breaches
Editor: Marianna Hardy
ISBN: 978-1-63321-269-5

Chapter 5

TESTIMONY OF JOHN MULLIGAN, EXECUTIVE VICE PRESIDENT AND CFO, TARGET CORPORATION. HEARING ON "PRIVACY IN THE DIGITAL AGE: PREVENTING DATA BREACHES AND COMBATING CYBERCRIME"*

I. INTRODUCTION

Good morning Chairman Leahy, Ranking Member Grassley, and Members of the Committee. My name is John Mulligan and I am the Executive Vice President and Chief Financial Officer of Target. I appreciate the opportunity to be here today to discuss important issues surrounding data breaches and cybercrime.

As you know, Target recently experienced a data breach resulting from a criminal attack on our systems. To begin, I want to say how deeply sorry we are for the impact this incident has had on our guests – your constituents. We know this breach has shaken their confidence in Target, and we are determined to work very hard to earn it back.

At Target we take our responsibility to our guests very seriously, and this attack has only strengthened our resolve. We will learn from this incident and

* This is an edited, reformatted and augmented version of testimony presented February 4, 2014 before a hearing of the Senate Judiciary Committee.

as a result, we hope to make Target, and our industry, more secure for consumers in the future.

I'd now like to explain the events of the breach as I currently understand them. Please recognize that I may not be able to provide specifics on certain matters because the criminal and forensic investigations remain active and ongoing. We are working closely with the U.S. Secret Service and the U.S. Department of Justice on the investigation – to help them bring to justice the criminals who perpetrated this wide-scale attack on Target, American business and consumers.

II. What We Know

On the evening of December 12, we were notified by the Justice Department of suspicious activity involving payment cards used at Target stores. We immediately started our internal investigation.

On December 13, we met with the Justice Department and the Secret Service. On December 14, we hired an independent team of experts to lead a thorough forensic investigation.

On December 15, we confirmed that criminals had infiltrated our system, had installed malware on our point-of-sale network and had potentially stolen guest payment card data. That same day, we removed the malware from virtually all registers in our U.S. stores.

Over the next two days, we began notifying the payment processors and card networks, preparing to publicly notify our guests and equipping our call centers and stores with the necessary information and resources to address the concerns of our guests.

On December 18 we disabled malware on about 25 additional registers which were disconnected from our system when we completed the initial malware removal on December 15. As a result, we determined that fewer than 150 additional guest accounts were affected.

Our actions leading up to our public announcement on December 19 – and since – have been guided by the principle of serving our guests, and we have been moving as quickly as possible to share accurate and actionable information with the public. When we announced the intrusion on December 19 we used multiple forms of communication, including a mass-scale public announcement, email, prominent notices on our website, and social media channels.

What we know today is that the breach affected two types of data: payment card data which affected approximately 40 million guests and certain personal data which affected up to 70 million guests. The theft of the payment card data affected guests who shopped at our U.S. stores from November 27 through December 18. The theft of partial personal data included name, mailing address, phone number or email address.

We now know that the intruder stole a vendor's credentials to access our system and place malware on our point-of-sale registers. The malware was designed to capture payment card data from the magnetic strip of credit and debit cards prior to encryption within our system.

As the forensic investigation continued, we learned that the malware also captured some strongly encrypted PIN data. We publicly shared this information on December 27, reassuring our guests that they would not be responsible for any fraudulent charges that may occur as a result of the breach.

When we subsequently confirmed the theft of partial personal data on January 9, we used various channels of communication to notify our guests on January 10 and provide them with tips to guard against possible scams.

III. Protecting Our Guests

From the outset, our response to the breach has been focused on supporting our guests and strengthening our security. In addition to the immediate actions I already described, we are taking the following concrete actions:

- First, we are undertaking an end-to-end review of our entire network and will make security enhancements, as appropriate.
- Second, we increased fraud detection for our Target REDcard guests. To date, we have not seen any fraud on our Target proprietary credit and debit cards due to this breach. And we have seen only a very low amount of additional fraud on our Target Visa card.
- Third, we are reissuing new Target credit or debit cards immediately to any guest who requests one.
- Fourth, we are offering one year of free credit monitoring and identity theft protection to anyone who has ever shopped at our U.S. Target stores. This protection includes a free credit report, daily credit monitoring, identity theft insurance and unlimited access to personalized assistance from a highly trained fraud resolution agent.

- Fifth, we informed our guests that they have zero liability for any fraudulent charges on their cards arising from this incident. We encouraged them to monitor their accounts and promptly alert either Target or their issuing bank of any suspicious activity.
- Sixth, Target is accelerating our investment in chip technology for our Target REDcards and stores' point-of-sale terminals. We believe that chip-enabled technologies are critical to providing enhanced protection for consumers, which is why we are a founding, and steering committee, member of the EMV Migration Forum at the SmartCard Alliance.
- Seventh, Target initiated the creation of, and is investing $5 million in, a campaign with Better Business Bureau, the National Cyber Security Alliance and the National Cyber- Forensics & Training Alliance to advance public education around cybersecurity and the dangers of consumer scams.
- And, eighth, last week Target helped launch a retail industry Cybersecurity and Data Privacy Initiative that will be focused on informing public dialogue and enhancing practices related to cybersecurity, improved payment security and consumer privacy. Target will be an active leader in this effort.

For many years, Target has invested significant capital and resources in security technology, personnel and processes. We had in place multiple layers of protection, including firewalls, malware detection software, intrusion detection and prevention capabilities and data loss prevention tools. We perform internal and external validation and benchmarking assessments. And, as recently as September 2013, our systems were certified as compliant with the Payment Card Industry Data Security Standards.

But, the unfortunate reality is that we suffered a breach, and all businesses – and their customers -- are facing increasingly sophisticated threats from cyber criminals. In fact, recent news reports have indicated that several other companies have been subjected to similar attacks.

IV. Moving Forward

To prevent this from happening again, none of us can go it alone. We need to work together.

Updating payment card technology and strengthening protections for American consumers is a shared responsibility and requires a collective and coordinated response. On behalf of Target, I am committing that we will be an active part of that solution.

Senators -- to each of you, and to all of your constituents and our guests, I want to say once again how sorry we are that this has happened. We will work with you, the business community, and other thought leaders to find effective solutions to this ongoing and pervasive challenge. Thank you very much for your time today.

In: The Target Store Data Breaches
Editor: Marianna Hardy
ISBN: 978-1-63321-269-5

Chapter 6

TESTIMONY OF MICHAEL R. KINGSTON, SENIOR VICE PRESIDENT AND CIO, THE NEIMAN MARCUS GROUP. HEARING ON "PRIVACY IN THE DIGITAL AGE: PREVENTING DATA BREACHES AND COMBATING CYBERCRIME"*

Mr. Chairman, Senator Grassley, members of the Committee, I want to thank you for your invitation to appear today to share with you our experiences regarding the recent criminal cybersecurity incident at our company.

For over 20 years, I have held numerous positions in the information technology field, and since April 2012 I have been proud to serve as Chief Information Officer of Neiman Marcus Group. We are in the midst of an ongoing forensic investigation that has revealed a cyber attack using very sophisticated malware. From the moment I learned that there might be a compromise of payment card information at our company, I have personally led the effort, in conjunction with others in senior management, outside consultants, and counsel, to ensure that we were acting swiftly, thoroughly, and responsibly to determine whether such a compromise had occurred, to protect our customers and the security of our systems, and to assist law enforcement in capturing the criminals. Because our investigation is ongoing, I

---

* This is an edited, reformatted and augmented version of testimony presented February 4, 2014 before a hearing of the Senate Judiciary Committee.

may be limited in my ability to speak definitively or with specificity on some issues, and there may be some questions to which I do not have the answers. Nevertheless, it is important to us as a company to make ourselves available to you to provide whatever information we can, as you attempt to address this important problem that confronts so many corporate and governmental entities around the world.

INTRODUCTION

Our company was founded 107 years ago. One of our founding principles is based on delivering exceptional service to our customers and building long lasting relationships with them that have spanned generations. We take this commitment to our customers very seriously. It is part of who we are and what we do daily to distinguish ourselves from other retailers.

We have never before been subjected to any sort of significant cybersecurity intrusion, so we have been particularly disturbed by this incident. It is clear that we are not alone, and that numerous retailers and others in the United States have been recently subjected to sophisticated attacks on their computer systems in an attempt to steal their customers' payment card information. The problem is clearly widespread. And the sophistication of these unprecedented cyber attacks makes the problem very challenging.

Through our ongoing forensic investigation, we have learned that the malware which penetrated our system was exceedingly sophisticated, a conclusion the Secret Service has confirmed with us. The malware was evidently able to capture payment card data in real time right after a card was swiped, and had sophisticated features that made it particularly difficult to detect. These features included some that were specifically customized to evade our multi- layered security architecture that provided strong protection of our systems and customer data. Our security measures included numerous firewalls at the corporate and store level, network segmentation, a customized tokenization tool, numerous encryption methods, an intrusion detection system, a two-factor authentication requirement, and use of industry-standard and centrally-managed enterprise anti-virus software. However, no system – no matter how sophisticated – is completely immune from cyber attack. A recent report prepared by the Secret Service and others in federal law enforcement crystallized the problem when they concluded that comparable

RAM scraping malware (perhaps less sophisticated than the one in our case, according to our investigators) had a *zero percent* anti-virus detection rate.

Because of the malware's sophisticated anti-detection devices, we did not learn that we had an actual problem in our computer system until *January 2*, and it was not until *January 6* when the malware and its outputs had been disassembled and decrypted enough that we were able to determine how it operated. Then, disabling it to ensure it was not still operating took until *January 10.* That day we sent out our first notices to customers potentially affected and made widely-reported public statements describing what we knew at that point about the incident.

Simply put, prior to January 2, despite our immediate efforts to have two separate firms of forensic investigators dig into our systems in an attempt to find any data security compromise, no data security compromise in our systems had been identified. A more detailed chronology of the period before January 2 is set out later in my testimony, but specifically:

Tues. Dec. 17: We receive a "CPP report" from MasterCard showing 122 payment cards with confirmed fraud use, suggesting that the "common point of purchase" (CPP) *may* have been one Neiman Marcus store where these cards had been previously used over a several-month period.

Wed. Dec. 18: We call forensic investigative firms in order to start an investigation, consistent with the card brand protocol. A new CPP report is received showing 74 cards.

Fri. Dec. 20: We hire a leading forensic investigative firm to conduct a thorough investigation. They start immediately. A new CPP report is received showing 26 cards.

Mon. Dec. 23: We notify federal law enforcement. They follow up with us shortly thereafter and we have been working with them since then. A new CPP report is received showing 2,185 cards.

Sun. Dec. 29: The forensic investigation has not turned up any evidence of a data compromise, and we decide to bring on a second leading forensic investigative firm to accelerate the investigation and help us determine whether we have a problem.

Wed. Jan. 1: For the first time, the forensic investigators find preliminary indications of malware that may have the capability to "scrape" or capture payment card data. This is confirmed on January 2, but it remains unknown whether the malware was able to function on our systems.

Mon. Jan. 6: After days of highly technical work disassembling, decrypting, and decoding the malware and its output files, the investigators conclude that the malware appeared to have been capturing payment card data at numerous stores. The immediate focus of the Neiman Marcus team turns to containing and disabling the malware as it is unknown whether the malware is still capturing card data.

Fri. Jan. 10: The malware appears to be contained and disabled. Neiman Marcus issues public statements identifying the data security incident and begins sending notices to customers on the CPP reports. Prominent coverage follows. We subsequently send out additional notices on our website and to all customers who shopped in any Neiman Marcus store or website during 2013, whether or not potentially exposed to the malware.

Based on the current state of the evidence in the ongoing investigation: (i) it now appears that the customer information that was potentially exposed to the malware was payment card account information from transactions in 77 of our 85 stores between July and October 2013, at different time periods within this date range in each store; (ii) we have no indication that transactions on our websites or at our restaurants were compromised; (iii) PIN data was not compromised, as we do not have PIN pads and do not request PINs; and (iv) there is no indication that social security numbers or other personal information were exposed in any way.

The policies of payment card brands protect our customers from any liability for any unauthorized charges if the fraudulent charges are reported in a timely manner. Nonetheless, we have now offered to any customer who shopped with us in the last year at either Neiman Marcus Group stores or websites – whether their card was exposed to the malware or not – one year of free credit monitoring and identity-theft insurance. We will continue to provide the excellent service to our customers that is our hallmark, and I know that the way we responded to this situation is consistent with that commitment.

December: CPP Reports and Forensic Investigation

This malware was discovered as a result of forensic investigative efforts by two of the leading computer forensic firms, hired by us upon receiving very limited information suggesting that there might have been a compromise regarding payment card data.

Specifically, on the evening of Friday, December 13, we were contacted by our merchant processor that Visa had identified an unknown number of fraudulently-reported credit cards with a possible common point of purchase at a small number of Neiman Marcus stores. The merchant processor provided no details concerning the number of cards affected, the credit card account numbers, or prior Neiman Marcus transactions. This initial report did not provide any indication of a cyber-incident or that our network may have been penetrated, but because even this limited information raised a potential concern, we immediately began an internal investigation to determine what could be responsible for the card fraud and whether our systems had been compromised in any way.

Despite repeated requests to our merchant processor over that weekend and on Monday for more information, we did not receive any additional information until Tuesday, December 17. On that date, we received a Common Point of Purchase ("CPP") report listing 122 MasterCard cards that had been used in one Neiman Marcus store and had subsequently been used fraudulently elsewhere.[1]

On December 18, we received another CPP report, this one listing 74 Visa cards. That day, consistent with Visa's protocols, we began contacting forensic investigative firms. On December 20, we engaged a leading forensic investigative firm to immediately start a thorough investigation of our systems in order to determine whether there was any evidence of a data compromise that might indicate the potential theft of payment card data.

Also on December 20, we received additional CPP reports listing a total of 26 Visa and MasterCard cards, bringing the total number of cards on the CPP reports to 222, which had been used at Neiman Marcus over a period of several months. Although we take any indication of potential payment-card theft seriously, this appeared to be a very small number of cards on CPP reports, especially in light of the millions of transactions Neiman Marcus Group conducts annually. News of the Target data security incident and its potential effect on 40 million payment cards was being reported, and this added to the uncertainty about whether the source of any payment card theft was within our system. And we had not received any CPP reports listing any American Express or Neiman Marcus private label credit card accounts.

On Monday, December 23, we received another CPP report which listed 2,185 MasterCard accounts relating to transactions at numerous Neiman Marcus stores. That day, we notified federal law enforcement of the situation, even though the forensic investigators had not found anything significant. In addition to giving them notice of our situation, we wanted to see if they could shed any light on areas where we should focus our attention and to determine if they had seen anything in their other investigations that would assist us in determining whether a compromise had occurred. The Secret Service followed up with us shortly thereafter, and we have been working closely with them since then.

Meanwhile, the investigation continued but was not turning up any evidence of a data compromise. This forensic work involved, among other things, experienced computer investigators looking at hundreds of thousands of files, logs, and other items of data in our system in an attempt to find anything out of the ordinary. However, by December 28, after a week of forensic investigative work, it was still not clear whether there was a problem in our system.

The next day, December 29, we decided to bring in a second leading computer forensic investigative firm to begin conducting an additional, independent investigation. Although the first firm had not found any evidence of a data compromise in our system that appeared in any way related to the potential theft of credit card information, we wanted another expert team to examine our system. Simply put, we wanted to accelerate the investigation and ensure that we were taking the best steps to protect our customers and to learn if our systems had been compromised.

January: Discovery and Containment of the Malware, and Notice to the Public and Our Customers

On January 1, the first investigative firm reported that they had discovered malware that they suspected to have card "scraping" functionality (malware that attempts to fraudulently obtain or capture payment card data). On January 2, the investigators reported that the malware appeared to actually have this functionality. However, they could not say whether the malware had functioned at all in our system, whether it had the capability to successfully capture and exfiltrate card data (that is, send data to an outside source), or whether exfiltration had actually occurred. For the next several days, the two investigative firms engaged in the difficult work of trying to learn what they could about the malware and look for evidence of its operation in different parts of our systems.

Attempting to figure out how the malware functioned was complicated work, requiring the investigators to disassemble the malware program and run tests in our technology labs to try to recreate its functionality. After some time they determined that the malware's output files were encrypted. They then developed a custom decoder to decrypt the output files. They also created a custom-coded scanning tool to determine where and how the malware was operating.

By January 6, we had succeeded in decrypting the output files and in locating the malware at various points on our system. As a result, certain observations about the malware could be made for the first time: the malware apparently operated at point-of-sale registers in multiple stores, and it appeared to have been successful in "scraping" and capturing payment card data at the moment a card is swiped through our Point of Sale system. However, it was unknown whether the malware had actually managed to steal data, the dates when it had been operating, and the full scope of how and where it had been operating.

In addition, our expert computer forensic investigators told us that the malware was highly sophisticated and was different than any other malware they had ever analyzed. Its complex, specialized elements helped to explain how the malware had successfully evaded detection, despite all of the security measures we had in place, in at least five different ways. First, the malware was apparently not known to the anti-virus community and had been written to evade anti-virus signatures. Second, the malware erased its tracks by removing the disk file that had caused it to run, even while the program itself was still running in memory – a highly unusual and difficult-to-achieve feature. Third, when the malware scraped and captured card data, it created encrypted output files, so the output files did not exhibit evidence of card-scraping activity – until they were decrypted. Fourth, the malware appeared to have features that were custom-built as a result of reconnaissance efforts within our systems that appear to have been clandestinely conducted earlier in 2013. Finally, the malware carefully covered its tracks with a built-in capability that wiped out files evidencing its operation by overwriting them with random data – making forensic detection much more difficult.

Although the investigators knew more about the malware by January 6, they did not know whether the malware was still scraping and capturing card data, and they were concerned that additional customer card data might be getting captured on an ongoing basis. The investigators discussed with us an immediate problem: since the malware was not yet contained, if the attacker learned that we had discovered the malware, there was a significant risk that the attacker might accelerate efforts to obtain captured account numbers, or that other cyber criminals might be encouraged to test our systems for vulnerabilities. Thus, our top priority at that point became disabling the malware.

From January 7 through January 10, we took a variety of steps in an attempt to ensure that the malware could not function. Since we did not yet know the full contours of how the malware functioned, designing a containment strategy was highly challenging. Nevertheless, by January 10, the investigators had a substantial level of confidence that the malware had been disabled.

That day, January 10, Neiman Marcus announced publicly that we had suffered a data security incident and that some customers' payment card information had been potentially compromised. This announcement was widely disseminated by the media in prominent print and broadcast coverage, and appeared on social media. We also sent email notices that same day to all customers whose payment cards were listed on the CPP reports (about 2,400) for whom we had email addresses. The next business day we sent letter notices to all customers in that group for whom we had postal addresses.

On January 16, our CEO Karen Katz issued a public letter, posted on our website with a prominent link from our home page, explaining that we had been the subject of a data security incident, and offering free credit monitoring and identity-theft insurance for one year to any customer who had used any payment card to conduct any transaction during the past year at any Neiman Marcus Group store or website.

Around this time, the investigators became confident that the dates during which the card-scraping malware had been active was July 16 to October 30, 2013. The number of unique payment cards used at all Neiman Marcus Group stores during this period was approximately 1,100,000. However, the ongoing investigations have not found evidence of the malware operating in all Neiman Marcus Group stores, and it appears that the malware was probably not operating each day during this period based on current evidence. Thus, the number of payment cards that were potentially exposed during this period appears to be lower than 1,100,000, although we have not yet determined how much lower. Because the investigation is ongoing, this information is preliminary.

On January 22, we issued an updated public notice on our website explaining the July 16 – October 30 period and stating that 1,100,000 payment card accounts were potentially exposed. The same day, we sent out individual email and letter notices about the incident to any customer who used a payment card at any time in the past year for any Neiman Marcus Group purchase – whether in one of our stores or on our websites – and for whom we had address information. Our individual notices again provided information about the offer of free credit monitoring and identity-theft insurance.

Notably, we sent this notice – and offered free credit monitoring and identity-theft insurance – to a much larger group than the cardholders whose information appears to have been potentially exposed. Our expanded group included anyone who had used a payment card over a much longer period of time (one year), and website customers (who do not appear to have been exposed to the malware). We took these steps in an abundance of caution because of the ongoing nature of the investigation, and because we want all of our customers to know that we place the highest priority on the security of their personal information.

THE ONGOING INVESTIGATION

As with other investigations, computer forensic investigations into data security incidents evolve over time, sometimes in unpredictable ways. We remain in close contact with law enforcement. My statements today are based on the current evidence from the investigations into this recent incident, and therefore should be considered tentative and subject to change. But even though we are still in the midst of discovering the facts, we are pleased to have had the opportunity to provide information to this Committee.

Thank you for your invitation to testify today, and I look forward to answering your questions.

End Note

[1] As we understand the general practice, accounts listed on CPP reports are accounts for which the issuing bank and the cardholder are both already aware that the card has been used fraudulently. These CPP reports provide some indication that a particular merchant *may* have a compromise regarding payment card data, based on analysis by the banks and the card brands. This analysis is tentative, not definitive. The reports indicate a level of suspicion that a problem may exist but do not establish that there actually is a problem, or the nature of the problem – including whether the potential theft of the cards relates to cybercrime or more traditional criminal methods. Nevertheless, our internal investigation focused on this information immediately.

In: The Target Store Data Breaches
Editor: Marianna Hardy

ISBN: 978-1-63321-269-5

Chapter 7

TESTIMONY OF FRAN ROSCH, SENIOR VICE PRESIDENT, SECURITY PRODUCTS AND SERVICES, ENDPOINT AND MOBILITY, SYMANTEC CORPORATION. HEARING ON "PRIVACY IN THE DIGITAL AGE: PREVENTING DATA BREACHES AND COMBATING CYBERCRIME"*

Chairman Leahy, Ranking Member Grassley, distinguished members of the Committee, thank you for the opportunity to testify today on behalf of Symantec Corporation.

My name is Fran Rosch, and I am the Senior Vice President, Security Products and Services, Endpoint and Mobility at Symantec. In this role I drive the development and execution of Symantec and Norton's endpoint and mobile management and protection strategy. I joined Symantec in 2010 through the acquisition of VeriSign's security business, and during my twelve-year career with VeriSign I worked with the company's largest customers to design and deploy effective security solutions to solve business challenges.

Symantec protects much of the world's information, and is a global leader in security, backup and availability solutions. Symantec is the largest security

* This is an edited, reformatted and augmented version of testimony presented February 4, 2014 before a hearing of the Senate Judiciary Committee.

software company in the world, with over 31 years of experience developing Internet security technology and helping consumers, businesses and governments secure and manage their information and identities. Our products and services protect people and information in any environment – from the smallest mobile device, to the enterprise data center, to cloud-based systems. We have established some of the most comprehensive sources of Internet threat data in the world through our Global Intelligence Network, which is comprised of millions of attack sensors, and we maintain 10 Security Response Centers. These sensors record thousands of events per second. In addition, every day we process billions of e-mail messages and web requests across our 14 global data centers. These resources allow us to capture worldwide security intelligence data that give our analysts a unique view of the entire Internet threat landscape.

The hearing today is not only timely – given the recent high profile data breaches – but it is a critically important discussion that will help focus attention on what businesses can do to protect themselves from similar attacks. Symantec welcomes the opportunity to provide comments to the Committee as it looks at how to prevent data breaches, combat cybercrime, and protect privacy.

In my testimony today, I will discuss:

- The need for basic computer hygiene;
- Recent statistics on data breaches;
- How breaches are happening, including the methods criminals are using to steal data;
- Security measures to protect data and prevent breaches; and
- Key elements for data breach legislation.

COMPUTER HYGIENE AS A BASIC LAYER OF DEFENSE

Preventing data breaches and protecting privacy starts with basic computer hygiene such as having security software installed, good patch management practices, using strong passwords, and not responding to suspicious emails. But that is just the start, because sophisticated, well-funded attackers are persistent and highly skilled. Anti-virus software (AV) should be part of any security program and will stop known malicious software (malware), but it is just one element. Today, even moderately sophisticated pieces of malware have unique signatures and can slip past systems that are using only AV software. Thus, strong security is layered security – in addition to basic computer hygiene and AV software, organizations need comprehensive protection that includes intrusion protection, reputation-based security, behavioral-based blocking, and data loss prevention tools. These advanced tools look not just for known threats, but they can check the reputation of any file that is loaded on a computer and look for other behavior that could indicate the presence of previously unknown malware.

The kinds of attacks on point-of-sale (PoS) devices that this hearing is looking at are not new, but it does appear the pace is increasing. The increase in successful attacks brings with it media attention and citizen concern, but it is critically important that the public conversation we are now having *not* just be about one attack or one company. Every retailer is at risk, and over time we often learn that the most widely reported victim was not the one hit hardest. So the conversation should be about breaches – plural – not just one breach; it should be about how they are happening, how government can go after the sophisticated criminal enterprises that steal the data, and what organizations can do to prevent and minimize the risk of a successful attack.

DATA BREACHES BY THE NUMBERS

For organizations that have critical information assets such as customer data, intellectual property, trade secrets, and proprietary corporate data, the risk associated with a data breach is now higher than ever before. Simply put, stealing data is big business; most major breaches are part of sophisticated criminal enterprises that trade on stolen identities and credit card numbers. The cost impacts of and the metrics associated with worldwide data breaches are significant.

In 2013, we estimate that the identities of over 435 million people were exposed, and that number is rising as new reports surface. For comparison, our estimate for 2012 was 93 million, and for 2011 was 232 million.[1] In fact, a recent report by the Online Trust Alliance indicates that of the top ten breaches in history, 40% occurred in 2013.[2] Of course, the total number of identities exposed is cumulative – once a person's identity has been exposed, it does not get "unexposed" when the calendar changes. So in the most basic of terms, as a result of breaches over the past three years, the personal information of up to 750 million individuals is or could be for sale on the criminal black market to be used for identity theft, credit card fraud, and countless other illegal activities.

It is important to remember that not every one of these victims will have his or her identity stolen or bank account raided. In fact, a low percentage of them will actually suffer that kind of direct loss. But every one of them is at risk for it because once your personal information is outside of your control your options are limited. You can start credit monitoring and get new credit cards, but to a large degree your best hope is that the information becomes stale before someone tries to use it themselves or sell it on the thriving black market.

The cost of these breaches is very real and is borne directly by both consumers and organizations:

- In our 2013 Norton Report, we estimated the global price tag of consumer cybercrime was $113 billion annually;[3]
- We estimate that there are 378 million victims of consumer cybercrime per year (1 million victims per day, 12 per second);[4]
- The Ponemon Institute estimates that in 2012, the cost to US companies was $188 per identity compromised;[5]
- Ponemon's survey concluded that the average total cost of a breach in 2012 was $5.4 million;[6] and
- Attackers are increasingly targeting smaller businesses, 71% of which say their operations are somewhat or very dependent on the Internet.[7]

The Ponemon survey also found that an ounce of prevention is worth a pound of cure. Strong security protocols before a breach and good incident management policies can dramatically cut the cost of a breach. Similarly, more consumers than ever are taking basic security measures such as using security software and deleting suspicious emails.

How Data Breaches Are Occurring

While the continuing onslaught of data breaches is well documented, what is less understood is why data breaches happen and what can be done to prevent them. The main causes for breaches are targeted attacks and human error.

Targeted attacks are indeed an increasing cause of data breaches. According to our 2013 Internet Security Threat Report (ISTR), 40% of data breaches were caused by hackers.[8] Some are direct attacks on a company's servers, where attackers search for unpatched vulnerabilities on websites or undefended connections to the Internet. But most rely on social engineering – in the simplest of terms, tricking people into doing something they would not do if fully aware of the consequences of their actions. Email is still a major attack vector and can take the form of broad mailings ("phishing") or highly targeted messages ("spear phishing"). More and more we see the latter variety, with publicly available information used to craft an email designed to dupe a specific victim or group of victims. The goal of both varieties is to get victims to open an infected file or go to a malicious or compromised website. While good security will stop most of these attacks – which often seek to exploit older, known vulnerabilities – many organizations do not have up-to-date security, do not make full use of the security tools available to them, or have it unevenly applied throughout their enterprise.

Another major cause of breaches is a lack of basic computer hygiene practices, often in the form of company employees who do not follow data security policies. Even today – despite the recent focus on the loss of personal information – a large segment of the workforce handles sensitive information on unprotected mobile devices, servers, desktops, and laptops. Ironically, in many ways this is the natural result of a highly productive workforce. One of the most common types of data breach occurs when sensitive data that an employee stores, sends, or copies is not encrypted. If a laptop is lost or stolen – or a hacker gains access to a network – these files are left unprotected. And while most large companies have policies requiring encryption or other security precautions for sensitive data, many employees either do not have the tools available or they ignore or are unaware of the policies.

Email, web mail, and removable storage devices are another major source of breaches. Most of us at one time or another have emailed something to our personal email address from our office so that we can work on it later. If our email accounts or home computers are compromised, or if we misplace the thumb drive we use to transport files, any sensitive, unencrypted data we sent is now lost and our company has had a data breach. Data breaches also can occur through outright theft, often by a fired or disgruntled employee.

Cybercriminals are also targeting the places where we "live and play" online in order to get at sensitive personal data. Social media is an increasingly sinister tool for cybercriminals. It is particularly effective in direct attacks, as people tend to trust things that appear to come from a friend's social media feed. But social media is also widely used to conduct reconnaissance for spear phishing or other targeted attacks; it often provides just the kind of personal details that a skilled attacker can use to get a victim to let his or her guard down. The old cliché is true when it comes to cyber attacks: we have to be right 100% of the time in protecting ourselves, while the attacker only has to get it right once.

We are also seeing the rapid growth of "watering hole" attacks on Internet sites. Like the lion in the wild who stalks a watering hole for unsuspecting prey, cybercriminals have become adept at lying in wait on legitimate websites and using them to try to infect visitors' computers. They do so by compromising legitimate websites that their victims are likely to visit and modifying them so that they will surreptitiously try to deliver malware to every visitor. For example, one attacker targeted mobile app developers by compromising a site that was popular with them. In another case, we saw employees from 500 different companies visit one compromised site in just 24 hours, each running the risk of infection.[9] Cybercriminals gain control of these websites through many of the same tactics described above – spear phishing and other social engineering attacks on the site managers, developers, or owners. Many of these websites were compromised through known attack vectors, meaning that good security practices could have prevented them from being compromised, and sensitive data on users systems would have been protected.

All of these attacks have essentially one goal: to get control of the user's computer, because once they have gained this foothold they can use the system for virtually any criminal purpose (including stealing data). When infiltrating a company, once inside, attackers typically will conduct reconnaissance of the system and then move laterally within it until they find what they want to take. In the case of a retailer, this can include compromising PoS devices and stealing information in bulk from them. In the case of an attack on an individual, the criminal will install malware that allows them to steal information or otherwise take control of the computer for future use.

PROTECTING DATA AND PREVENTING BREACHES

Basic Security Steps - i.e., Closing the Door

When it comes to security, it starts with the basics. Though criminals' tactics are continually evolving, good cyber hygiene, as discussed previously, is still the simplest and most cost-effective first step. Strong passwords remain the foundation of good security – on home and work devices, email, social media accounts, or whatever you use to communicate (or really anything you log into). And these passwords must be different, because using a single password means that a breach of one account exposes all of your accounts. Using a second authentication factor (whether through a text message, a smart card, biometrics, or a token with a changing numeric password) significantly increases the security of a login.

Patch management is also critical. Individuals and organizations should not delay installing patches, or software updates, because the same patch that closes a vulnerability on one computer can be a roadmap for a criminal to exploit that vulnerability and compromise any unpatched devices. The reality is that a large percentage of computers around the world, including some in large organizations, do not get patched regularly, and cybercriminals count on this. While so-called "zero day exploits" – previously unknown critical vulnerabilities – get the most press, it is older, unpatched vulnerabilities that cause most systems to get compromised.

Modern Security Software – i.e., Bolting the Doors and Windows

But poor or insufficiently deployed security can also lead to a breach, and a modern security suite that is being fully utilized is also essential. While most people still commonly refer to security software as "anti-virus" or AV, advanced security protection is much more than that. In the past, the same piece of malware would be delivered to thousands or even millions of computers. Today, cybercriminals can take the same malware and create unlimited unique variants that can slip past basic AV software. If all your security software does is check for signatures (or digital fingerprints) of known malware, you are by definition not protected against even moderately sophisticated attacks. Put differently, a check-the-box security program that only includes installation of basic AV software may give you piece of mind – but that is about all it will give you.

Modern security software does much more than look for known malware: it monitors your computer, watching for unusual internet traffic, activity, or system processes that could be indicative of malicious activity. At Symantec we also use what we call Insight and SONAR, which are reputation-based and behavior-based heuristic security technologies. Insight is a reputation-based technology that uses our Global Intelligence Network to put files in context, using their age, frequency, location and other characteristics to expose emerging threats that might otherwise be missed. If a computer is trying to execute a file that we have never seen anywhere in the world and that comes from an unknown source, there is a high probability that it is malicious – and Insight will either warn the user or block it. SONAR is behavior-based protection that uses proactive local monitoring to identify and block suspicious processes on computers.

Tailoring Security to the Device – i.e., Locking Your Valuables in a Safe

Security should also be specific to the device being protected, and in some ways PoS devices have advantages over other systems. For while a modern PoS system is typically at its core just a computer running a mainstream operating system, the functions it needs to perform can be narrowly defined. Because a user on such a device typically does not browse the web, send emails, or open shared drives, the functionally of the machine and the files that actually need to be on it are limited. This allows businesses to reduce the attack surface by locking down the system and using application control tools, as well as controlling which devices and applications are allowed to access the network. Doing so can render many strains of malware useless because they would not be allowed to run on the devices.

In addition, payment card system infrastructure is highly complex and threats can be introduced at any number of points within the system. The special report we released yesterday, Attacks on Point of Sales Systems, provides an overview of the methods that attackers may use to gain entry into a system.[10] It also describes the steps that retailers and other organizations can use to protect PoS systems and mitigate the risk of an attack.

Encrypting Data – i.e., Hiding Family Treasures in a Secret Compartment in Your Safe

Encryption also is key to protecting your most valuable data. Even the best security will not stop a determined attacker, and encrypting your sensitive data provides defense in breadth, or across many platforms. Good encryption ensures that any data stolen will be useless to virtually all cybercriminals. The bottom line in computer security is no different from physical security – nothing is perfect. We can make it hard, indeed very hard, for an attacker, but if resourced and persistent criminals want to compromise a particular company or site, with time they are probably going to find a way to do it. Good security means not just doing the utmost to keep them out, but also to recognize that you must take steps to limit any damage they can do should they get in.

RESPONDING TO A BREACH

The criminal organizations that carry out many of the major targeted attacks are well funded, sophisticated, and persistent. In the face of this onslaught, even the most security conscious organizations can have a data breach. Every organization needs to be prepared to manage the effects of one, because deploying an effective incident management plan after a breach can help mitigate the damage of the data loss. Organizations need to be prepared to react on several different fronts, beginning with an incident response team that represents all functional groups within an organization and a response plan that has been exercised before an incident has occurred. Lastly, organizations need to be prepared to bring in law enforcement and, as expeditiously as possible, notify anyone impacted and communicate timely information to them.

In the longer term, effective sharing of actionable information among the public and private sectors on cyber threats, vulnerabilities, and incidents is an essential component of improving overall cybersecurity and combatting cybercrime. At Symantec, we participate in various industry organizations, as well as public-private partnerships in the US and globally with all levels of government. We share high-level cybercrime and cyber threat trends and information on a voluntary basis through a number of different fora to help protect our customers and their networks. Among our partners are the National Cyber-Forensics and Training Alliance (NCFTA), which includes more than 80 industry partners and law enforcement from around the world, and the Information Technology (IT) Information Sharing and Analysis Center (ISAC), which is comprised of 27 leading IT vendors and contributes to cyber risk management of the other 15 critical infrastructure sectors through the National Council of ISACs.

DATA BREACH LEGISLATION

In the United States today, there are at least 48 state-specific data breach notification laws. This creates an enormous compliance burden, particularly for smaller companies, and does little to actually protect consumers. Symantec supports a national standard for data breach notification, built on three principles:

1. **Data security legislation should apply equally to all.** The scope of any legislation should include all entities that collect, maintain, or sell significant numbers of records containing sensitive personal information. Requirements should impact government and the private sector equally, and should include educational institutions and charitable organizations as well. By the same token, any new legislation should consider existing federal regulations that govern data breach for some sectors and not create duplicative, additional, or conflicting rules.
2. **Implementing pre-breach security measures should be a part of any legislation.** As the Ponemon survey demonstrates, breaches are much less costly for companies that are proactive. New legislation should not simply require notification of consumers in case of a data breach, but should seek to minimize the likelihood of a breach by pushing organizations to take reasonable security measures to ensure the confidentiality and integrity of sensitive personal information. Numerous standards, best practices, and guidelines already exist to help organizations establish a cybersecurity program or improve an existing one. The Cybersecurity Framework that NIST will issue next week is the result of a lengthy and successful public-private partnership and if it is consistent with the drafts we have seen will be a flexible, scalable tool that organizations of all sizes and sophistication levels can use to secure their environments and protect critical infrastructure.
3. **The use of encryption or other security measures that render data unreadable and unusable should be a key element in establishing the threshold for the need for notification.** Any notification scheme should minimize "false positives" – notices to individuals who are later shown *not* to have been impacted by a breach because their data was rendered unusable before it was stolen. A clear reference to the "usability" of information should be considered when determining whether notification is required in case of a breach. Promoting the use of encryption as a best practice would significantly reduce the number of "false positives," thus reducing the burden on consumers and business.

CONCLUSION

This hearing is a key part of an important conversation that we need to have as a nation. Data breaches and cyber threats are a part of every American's day-to-day lives, and will be even more so in the years to come. We will never be able to prevent every data breach or every cyber attack, but working together, industry and government can make it increasingly more difficult – and more expensive – for cybercriminals to succeed.

End Notes

[1] *Symantec Internet Security Threat Report* XVIII (April 2013), 17. http://www.symantec.com /security response/publications/threatreport.jsp
[2] *2014 OTA Data Breach Guide*, 4. https://otalliance.org/breach.html
[3] *2013 Norton Cybercrime Report* (October 2013), 8. http://www.symantec.com/about/news /resources/press kits/detail.jsp?pkid=norton-report-2013
[4] *Id.* at 10.
[5] *Cost of Data Breach Study: Global Analysis*, Ponemon Institute (May 2013), 1. http://www. symantec.com/about/news/resources/press kits/detail.jsp?pkid=ponemon-2013
[6] *Id.* at 1.
[7] *Symantec 2012 National Small Business Study Fact Sheet,* National Cybersecurity Alliance & Symantec Corporation, 1. http://www.staysafeonline.org/stay-safe-online/resources/
[8] *ISTR XVIII*, 19.
[9] *Id.* at 21.
[10] *Special Report on Attacks on Point of Sales Systems*, Symantec Security Response (February 2014). http://www.symantec.com/content/en/us/enterprise/media/security response/white papers/attacks on point of sale systems.pdf

In: The Target Store Data Breaches
Editor: Marianna Hardy

ISBN: 978-1-63321-269-5

Chapter 8

STATEMENT OF EDITH RAMIREZ, CHAIRWOMAN, FEDERAL TRADE COMMISSION. HEARING ON "PRIVACY IN THE DIGITAL AGE: PREVENTING DATA BREACHES AND COMBATING CYBERCRIME"*

I. INTRODUCTION

Chairman Leahy, Ranking Member Grassley, and members of the Committee, I am Edith Ramirez, Chairwoman of the Federal Trade Commission ("FTC" or "Commission").[1] I appreciate the opportunity to present the Commission's testimony on data security.

We live in an increasingly connected world, and information is the new currency. Businesses in this data-driven economy are collecting more personal information about consumers than ever before, and storing and transmitting across their own systems as well as the Internet. But, as recent publicly announced data breaches remind us,[2] these vast systems of data are susceptible to being compromised. Hackers and others seek to exploit vulnerabilities, obtain unauthorized access to consumers' sensitive information, and potentially misuse it in ways that can cause serious harms to consumers as well as businesses.

* This is an edited, reformatted and augmented version of a statement presented February 4, 2014 before a hearing of the Senate Judiciary Committee.

All of this takes place against the background of the threat of identity theft, a pernicious crime that harms both consumers and financial institutions. The Bureau of Justice Statistics estimates that 16.6 million persons – or 7 percent of all U.S. residents ages 16 and older – were victims of identity theft in 2012.[3]

As the nation's leading privacy enforcement agency, the FTC is committed to protecting consumer privacy and promoting data security in the private sector and has settled 50 law enforcement actions against businesses that we alleged failed to protect consumers' personal information appropriately. Data security is of critical importance to consumers. If companies do not protect the personal information they collect and store, that information could fall into the wrong hands, resulting in fraud and other harm, along with a potential loss of consumer confidence in particular business sectors or entities, payment methods, or types of transactions. Accordingly, the Commission has undertaken substantial efforts for over a decade to promote data security in the private sector through civil law enforcement, education, policy initiatives, and recommendations to Congress to enact legislation in this area. The FTC has also worked with the Department of Justice and criminal investigative agencies, as well as state Attorneys General, to coordinate efforts and leverage government resources more effectively.

The Commission is here today to reiterate its longstanding bipartisan call for enactment of a strong federal data security and breach notification law. Never has the need for legislation been greater. With reports of data breaches on the rise, and with a significant number of Americans suffering from identity theft, Congress needs to act. This testimony provides an overview of the Commission's efforts and restates the Commission's support for data security legislation.

II. The Commission's Data Security Program

A. Law Enforcement

To promote data security, the Commission enforces several statutes and rules that impose obligations upon businesses that collect and maintain consumer data. The Commission's Safeguards Rule, which implements the Gramm-Leach-Bliley Act ("GLB Act"), for example, provides data security requirements for non-bank financial institutions.[4] The Fair Credit Reporting Act ("FCRA") requires consumer reporting agencies to use reasonable procedures to ensure that the entities to which they disclose sensitive consumer information have a permissible purpose for receiving that information,[5] and imposes safe disposal obligations on entities that maintain consumer report information.[6] The Children's Online Privacy Protection Act ("COPPA") requires reasonable security for children's information collected online.[7]

In addition, the Commission enforces the proscription against unfair or deceptive acts or practices in Section 5 of the FTC Act. [8] If a company makes materially misleading statements or omissions about a matter, including data security, and such statements or omissions are likely to mislead reasonable consumers, they can be found to be deceptive in violation of Section 5.[9] Using its deception authority, the Commission has settled more than 30 matters challenging companies' express and implied claims that they provide reasonable security for consumers' personal data when, the Commission charged, the companies failed to employ available, cost-effective security measures to minimize or reduce data risks.

Further, if a company's data security practices cause or are likely to cause substantial injury to consumers that is neither reasonably avoidable by consumers nor outweighed by countervailing benefits to consumers or to competition, those practices can be found to be unfair and violate Section 5.[10] Congress expressly codified these criteria in Section 5.[11] The Commission has settled over 20 cases alleging that a company's failure to reasonably safeguard consumer data was an unfair practice.[12]

In the data security context, the FTC conducts its investigations with a focus on reasonableness – a company's data security measures must be reasonable in light of the sensitivity and volume of consumer information it holds, the size and complexity of its business, and the cost of available tools to improve security and reduce vulnerabilities. The Commission examines such factors as whether the risks at issue were well known or reasonably foreseeable, the costs and benefits of implementing various protections, and the tools that are currently available and used in the marketplace. This same reasonableness requirement is the basis for sectoral laws that have data security requirements, including the GLB Act and the FCRA.

Since 2001, the Commission has used its authority under these laws to settle 50 cases against businesses that it charged with failing to provide reasonable and appropriate protections for consumers' personal information.[13] The practices at issue were not merely isolated mistakes. In each of these cases, the Commission examined a company's practices as a whole and challenged alleged data security failures that were multiple and systemic. And through these settlements, the Commission has made clear that it does not require perfect security; that reasonable and appropriate security is a continuous process of assessing and addressing risks; that there is no one-size-fits-all data security program; and that the mere fact that a breach occurred does not mean that a company has violated the law.

In its most recent case, the FTC settled allegations that GMR Transcription Services, Inc., and its owners violated Section 5 of the FTC Act.[14] According to the complaint, GMR provides audio file transcription services for their clients, which include health care providers, and relies on service providers and independent typists to perform this work. GMR exchanged audio files and transcripts with customers and typists by loading them on a file server. As a result of GMR's alleged failure to implement reasonable and appropriate security measures or to ensure its service providers also implemented reasonable and appropriate security, at least 15,000 files containing sensitive personal information – including consumers' names, birthdates, and medical histories – were available to anyone on the Internet. The Commission's order resolving the case prohibits GMR from making misrepresentations about privacy and security, and requires the company to implement a comprehensive information security program and undergo independent audits for the next 20 years.

The FTC also recently announced its first data security settlement concerning the "Internet of Things" – *i.e.*, Internet-connected refrigerators, thermostats, cars, and many other products and devices which can communicate with each other and/or consumers. The TRENDnet settlement involved a video camera designed to allow consumers to monitor their homes remotely.[15] The complaint alleges that TRENDnet marketed its SecurView cameras for purposes ranging from home security to baby monitoring, and claimed in numerous product descriptions that they were "secure." However, the cameras had faulty software that left them open to online viewing, and in some instances listening, by anyone with the cameras' Internet address. This resulted in hackers posting 700 consumers' live feeds on the Internet. Under the FTC settlement, TRENDnet must maintain a comprehensive security program, obtain outside audits, notify consumers about the security issues and the availability of software updates to correct them, and provide affected customers with free technical support for the next two years.

Finally, the FTC has also brought a number of cases alleging that unreasonable security practices allowed hackers to gain access to consumers' credit and debit card information, leading to many millions of dollars of fraud loss.[16] For example, the Commission alleged that TJX's failure to use reasonable and appropriate security measures resulted in a hacker obtaining tens of millions of credit and debit payment cards, as well as the personal information of approximately 455,000 consumers who returned merchandise to the stores.[17] Banks also claimed that tens of millions of dollars in fraudulent charges were made, and cancelled and reissued millions of cards. Meanwhile, criminal law enforcement authorities investigated and prosecuted the hackers involved in this and other data breaches.[18] As this matter illustrates, the goals of FTC and federal criminal agencies are complementary: FTC actions send a message that businesses need to protect their customers' data on the front end, and actions by criminal agencies send a message to identity thieves that their efforts to victimize consumers will be punished.

B. Policy Initiatives

The Commission also undertakes policy initiatives to promote privacy and data security, including by hosting workshops on emerging business practices and technologies affecting consumer data. This testimony describes two such recent initiatives that addressed information security issues.

In November, the FTC held a workshop on the "Internet of Things."[19] The workshop brought together academics, industry representatives, and consumer advocates to explore the security and privacy issues from increased connectivity in everyday devices, in areas as diverse as smart homes, health and fitness devices, and cars.

Last June, the Commission hosted a public forum on mobile security issues, including potential threats to U.S. consumers and possible solutions to them.[20] As the use of mobile technology increases at a rapid rate and consumers take advantage of the technology's benefits in large numbers, it is important to address threats that exist today as well as those that may emerge in the future. The forum brought together technology researchers, industry members and academics to explore the security of existing and developing mobile technologies and the roles various members of the mobile ecosystem can play in protecting consumers from potential security threats.

The Commission has also hosted programs on emerging forms of identity theft, such as child identity theft[21] and senior identity theft.[22] In these programs, the Commission discussed unique challenges facing children and seniors, and worked with stakeholders to develop outreach messages and plans for these two communities. Since the workshops took place, the Commission has continued to engage in such tailored outreach.

C. Consumer Education and Business Guidance

The Commission also promotes better data security practices through consumer education and business guidance. On the consumer education front, the Commission sponsors OnGuard Online, a website designed to educate consumers about basic computer security.[23] OnGuard Online and its Spanish-language counterpart, Alerta en Línea,[24] average more than 2.2 million unique visits per year.

As directed by Congress, the Commission maintains the nation's main repository of identity theft complaints, housed within our Consumer Sentinel consumer complaint database, and provides centralized resources for victims of identity theft.[25] Identity theft has been the top consumer complaint to the FTC for 13 consecutive years, and tax identity theft – which often begins by thieves obtaining Social Security numbers and other personal information from consumers in order to obtain their tax refund – has been an increasing share of the Commission's identity theft complaints.[26] To address these concerns, Commission staff have worked with members of Congress to host numerous town hall meetings on identity theft in order to educate their constituents. And, just last month, the FTC hosted 16 events across the country, along with a series of national webinars and Twitter chats as part of Tax Identity Theft Awareness Week.[27] The events were designed to raise awareness about tax identity theft and provide consumers with tips on how to protect themselves, and what to do if they become victims. For consumers who may have been affected by the recent Target and other breaches, the FTC posted information online about steps they should take to protect themselves.[28]

The Commission directs its outreach to businesses as well. The FTC widely disseminates a business guide on data security, [29] along with an online tutorial based on the guide.[30] These resources are designed to provide diverse businesses – and especially small businesses – with practical, concrete advice as they develop data security programs and plans for their companies. The Commission has also released articles directed towards a non-legal audience regarding basic data security issues for businesses.[31] For example, because mobile applications ("apps") and devices often rely on consumer data, the FTC has developed specific security guidance for mobile app developers as they create, release, and monitor their apps.[32] The FTC also creates business educational materials on specific topics – such as the risks associated with peer-to-peer ("P2P") file-sharing programs and companies' obligations to protect consumer and employee information from these risks[33] and how to properly secure and dispose of information on digital copiers.[34]

III. DATA SECURITY LEGISLATION

The FTC supports federal legislation that would (1) strengthen its existing authority governing data security standards on companies and (2) require companies, in appropriate circumstances, to provide notification to consumers when there is a security breach.[35] Reasonable and appropriate security practices are critical to preventing data breaches and protecting consumers' data from identity theft and other harm. Where breaches occur, notifying consumers helps them protect themselves from any harm that is likely to be caused by the misuse of their data. For example, in the case of a breach of Social Security numbers, notifying consumers will enable them to request that fraud alerts be placed in their credit files, obtain copies of their credit reports, scrutinize their monthly account statements, and take other steps to protect themselves. And although most states have breach notification laws in place, having a strong and consistent national requirement would simplify compliance by businesses while ensuring that all consumers are protected.

Legislation in both areas – data security and breach notification – should give the FTC rulemaking authority under the Administrative Procedure Act, jurisdiction over non-profits, and the ability to seek civil penalties to help deter unlawful conduct. Enabling the FTC to bring cases against non-profits[36] would help ensure that whenever personal information is collected from consumers, entities that maintain such data adequately protect it.[37] In addition, under current laws, the FTC only has the authority to seek civil penalties for data security violations involving companies that fail to protect children's information provided online in violation of the COPPA Rule or credit report information in violation of the FCRA.[38] We urge Congress to allow the FTC to seek civil penalties against other companies to ensure that FTC actions can deter unreasonable data security practices in all appropriate instances.

CONCLUSION

Thank you for the opportunity to provide the Commission's views on data security. The FTC remains committed to promoting reasonable security for consumer data and we look forward to continuing to work with Congress on this critical issue.

End Notes

[1] This written statement presents the views of the Federal Trade Commission. My oral statements and responses to questions are my own and do not necessarily reflect the views of the Commission or of any other Commissioner.

[2] *See* Elizabeth A. Harris & Nicole Perlroth, *For Target, the Breach Numbers Grow*, N.Y. Times, Jan. 10, 2014, *available at* http://www.nytimes.com/2014/01/11/business/target- (discussing recently-announced breaches involving payment card information by Target and Neiman Marcus); Nicole Perlroth, *Michaels Stores Is Investigating Data Breach*, N.Y. Times, Jan. 25, 2014, *available at* http://www.nytimes.com/2014/01/26/technology/ (discussing Michaels Stores' announcement of potential security breach involving payment card information).

[3] *See* Bureau of Justice Statistics, *Victims of Identity Theft, 2012* (Dec. 2013), *available at* http://www.bjs.gov/content/pub/pdf/vit12.pdf.

[4] 16 C.F.R. Part 314, implementing 15 U.S.C. § 6801(b).

[5] 15 U.S.C. § 1681e.

[6] *Id.* at § 1681w. The FTC's implementing rule is at 16 C.F.R. Part 682.

[7] 15 U.S.C. §§ 6501-6506; *see also* 16 C.F.R. Part 312 ("COPPA Rule").

[8] 15 U.S.C. § 45(a).

[9] *See* Federal Trade Commission Policy Statement on Deception, *appended to Cliffdale Assocs., Inc.*, 103 F.T.C. 110, 174 (1984).

[10] *See* Federal Trade Commission Policy Statement on Unfairness, *appended to Int'l Harvester Co.*, 104 F.T.C. 949, 1070 (1984) ("FTC Unfairness Statement").

[11] 15 U.S.C. § 5(n).

[12] Some of the Commission's data security settlements allege both deception and unfairness.

[13] *See* Commission Statement Marking the FTC's 50th Data Security Settlement, Jan. 31, 2014, *available at* http://www.ftc.gov/system/files/documents/cases/140131gmrstatement.pdf.

[14] *GMR Transcription Servs., Inc..*, Matter No. 112-3120 (F.T.C. Dec. 16, 2013) (proposed consent order), *available at* http://www.ftc.gov/news-events/press-releases/2014/01 /provider-medical-transcriptservices-settles-ftc-charges-it.

[15] *TRENDnet, Inc.*, No. 122-3090 (Sept. 4, 2013), *available at* http://www.ftc.gov/opa/2013 /09/trendnet.shtm.

[16] *See, e.g.*, *Dave & Busters, Inc.*, No. C-4291 (F.T.C. May 20, 2010), *available at* http://www. ftc.gov/enforcement/ *DSW, Inc.*, No. C-4157 (F.T.C. Mar. 7, 2006), *available at* http://www.ftc.gov/enforcement/cases-andproceedings/cases/2006/03/dsw-incin-matter; *BJ's Wholesale Club, Inc.*, No. C-4148 (F.T.C. Sept. 20, 2005), *available at* http:// www.ftc.gov/enforcement/cases-and-proceedings/cases/2005/09/bjs-wholesaleclub-inc-matter.

[17] *The TJX Cos., Inc.*, No. C-4227 (F.T.C. July 29, 2008), *available at* http://www.ftc.gov/ enforcement

[18] *See, e.g.*, Kim Zetter, *TJX Hacker Gets 20 Years in Prison*, Wired, Mar. 25, 2010, *available at* http://www.wired.com/threatlevel/2010/03/tjx-sentencing

[19] FTC Workshop, *Internet of Things: Privacy & Security in a Connected World* (Nov. 19, 2013), *available at* http://www.ftc.gov/bcp/workshops/internet-of-things/.

[20] FTC Workshop, *Mobile Security: Potential Threats and Solutions* (June 4, 2013), *available at* http://www.ftc.gov/bcp/workshops/mobile-security

[21] FTC Workshop, *Stolen Futures: A Forum on Child Identity Theft* (July 12, 2011), *available at* http://www.ftc.gov/news-events/events-calendar/2011/07/stolen-futures-forum-child-identity

[22] FTC Workshop, *Senior Identity Theft: A Problem in This Day and Age* (May 7, 2013), *available at* http://www.ftc.gov/news-events/events-calendar/2013/05/senior-identity

[23] *See* http://www.onguardonline.gov.

[24] *See* http://www.alertaenlinea.gov.

[25] 18 U.S.C. § 1028 note.

[26] In 2012, tax identity theft accounted for more than 43% of the identity theft complaints, making it the largest category of identity theft complaints by a substantial margin. *See* Press Release, *FTC Releases Top 10 Complaint Categories for 2012* (Feb. 26, 2013), *available at* http://www.ftc.gov/newsevents/press-releases/2013/02/ftc-releases-top-10-complaint-categories-2012.

[27] Press Release, *FTC's Tax Identity Theft Awareness Week Offers Consumers Advice, Guidance* (Jan. 10, 2014), *available at* http://www.ftc.gov/news-events/press-releases/2014/01/ftcs-tax-identity-

[28] *See* Nicole Vincent Fleming, *An Unfortunate Fact About Shopping*, FTC Consumer Blog, http://www.consumer.ftc.gov/blog/unfortunate-fact-about-shopping (Jan. 27, 2014); Nicole Vincent Fleming, *Are you affected by the recent Target hack?*, FTC Consumer Blog, https://www.consumer.ftc.gov/blog/are-you-affected-recent-target. In addition to these materials posted in response to recent breaches, the FTC has long published a victim recovery guide and other resources to explain the immediate steps identity theft victims should take to address the crime; how to obtain a free credit report and correct fraudulent information in credit reports; how to file a police report; and how to protect their personal information. *See* http://www.consumer.ftc.gov/features/feature-0014- identity-theft.

[29] *See Protecting Personal Information: A Guide for Business*, *available at* http://business.ftc.gov/documents/bus69-protecting-personal-information-guide-business.

[30] *See Protecting Personal Information: A Guide for Business (Interactive Tutorial)*, *available at* http://business.ftc.gov/multimedia

[31] *See generally* http://www.business.ftc.gov/privacy-and-security

[32] *See Mobile App Developers: Start with Security* (Feb. 2013), *available at* http://business.ftc.gov/documents/bus83-mobile-app-developers-start-security

[33] *See Peer-to-Peer File Sharing: A Guide for Business* (Jan. 2010), *available at* http://business.ftc.gov/documents/bus46-peer-peer-file-sharing-guide-business.

[34] *See Copier Data Security: A Guide for Business* (Nov. 2010), *available at* http://business.ftc.gov/documents/bus43-copier-data-security

[35] *See, e.g.*, Prepared Statement of the Federal Trade Commission, "Privacy and Data Security: Protecting Consumers in the Modern World," Before the Senate Committee on Commerce, Science, and Transportation, 112th Cong., June 29, 2011, *available at* http://www.ftc.gov/sites/default/files/documents/public_statements/prepared-statement-federal-trade-commission-privacy-and-data-security Prepared Statement of the Federal Trade Commission, "Data Security," Before Subcommittee on Commerce, Manufacturing, and Trade of the House Committee on Energy and Commerce, 112th Cong., June 15, 2011, *available at* http://www.ftc.gov/sites/default/files/documents/public statements/prepared-statement-federal-trade-commission-data-security/110615datasecurityhouse.pdf; FTC, *Security in Numbers, SSNs and ID Theft* (Dec. 2008), *available at* http://www.ftc.gov/sites /default/files/documents/reports/security-numbers-social-security-numbers-andidentity-theft-federal-trade-commission-report/p075414ssnreport.pdf; President's Identity Theft Task Force, *Identity Theft Task Force Report* (Sept. 2008), *available at* http://www.ftc.gov/sites/default/files/documents/reports/presidents-identity-

[36] Non-profits are generally outside the FTC's jurisdiction. 15 U.S.C. §§ 44 & 45(a).

[37] A substantial number of reported breaches have involved non-profit universities and health systems. *See* Privacy Rights Clearinghouse Chronology of Data Breaches (listing breaches including breaches at non-profits, educational institutions, and health facilities), *available at* http://www.privacyrights.org/databreach/new.

[38] The FTC can also seek civil penalties for violations of administrative orders. 15 U.S.C. § 45(*l*).

In: The Target Store Data Breaches
Editor: Marianna Hardy
ISBN: 978-1-63321-269-5

Chapter 9

TESTIMONY OF WILLIAM NOONAN, DEPUTY SPECIAL AGENT IN CHARGE, CRIMINAL INVESTIGATIVE DIVISION, U.S. SECRET SERVICE. HEARING ON "PRIVACY IN THE DIGITAL AGE: PREVENTING DATA BREACHES AND COMBATING CYBERCRIME"[*]

Good afternoon Chairman Leahy, Ranking Member Grassley, and distinguished Members of the Committee. Thank you for the opportunity to testify on the risks and challenges the Nation faces from large-scale data breaches like those that have been recently reported and are of great concern to our Nation. The U.S. Secret Service (Secret Service) has decades of experience investigating large-scale criminal cyber intrusions, in addition to other crimes that impact our Nation's financial payment systems. Based on investigative experience and the understanding we have developed regarding transnational organized cyber criminals that are engaged in these data breaches and associated frauds, I hope to provide this committee useful insight into this issue from a federal law enforcement perspective to help inform your deliberations.

[*] This is an edited, reformatted and augmented version of testimony presented February 4, 2014 before a hearing of the Senate Judiciary Committee.

THE ROLE OF THE SECRET SERVICE

The Secret Service was founded in 1865 to protect the U.S. financial system from the counterfeiting of our national currency. As the Nation's financial system evolved from paper to plastic to electronic transactions, so too has the Secret Service's investigative mission. Today, our modern financial system depends heavily on information technology for convenience and efficiency. Accordingly, criminals have adapted their methods and are increasingly using cyberspace to exploit our Nation's financial payment system by engaging in fraud and other illicit activities. This is not a new trend; criminals have been committing cyber financial crimes since at least 1970.[1]

Congress established 18 USC § 1029-1030 as part of the Comprehensive Crime Control Act of 1984; these statutes criminalized unauthorized access to computers[2] and the fraudulent use or trafficking of access devices[3]—defined as any piece of information or tangible item that is a means of account access that can be used to obtain money, goods, services, or other thing of value.[4] Congress specifically gave the Secret Service authority to investigate violations of both statutes.[5]

Secret Service investigations have resulted in the arrest and successful prosecution of cyber criminals involved in the largest known data breaches, including those of TJ Maxx, Dave & Buster's, Heartland Payment Systems, and others. Over the past four years Secret Service cybercrime investigations have resulted in over 4,900 arrests, associated with approximately $1.37 billion in fraud losses and the prevention of over $11.24 billion in potential fraud losses. Through our work with our partners at the Department of Justice (DOJ), in particular the local U.S. Attorney Offices, the Computer Crimes and Intellectual Property section (CCIPS), the International Organized Crime Intelligence and Operations Center (IOC-2), and others, we are confident we will continue to bring the cyber criminals that perpetrate major data breaches to justice.

THE TRANSNATIONAL CYBERCRIME THREAT

Advances in computer technology and greater access to personally identifiable information (PII) via the Internet have created a virtual marketplace for transnational cyber criminals to share stolen information and criminal methodologies. As a result, the Secret Service has observed a marked increase in the quality, quantity, and complexity of cybercrimes targeting private industry and critical infrastructure. These crimes include network intrusions, hacking attacks, malicious software, and account takeovers leading to significant data breaches affecting every sector of the world economy. The recently reported data breaches of Target and Neiman Marcus are just the most recent, well-publicized examples of this decade-long trend of major data breaches perpetrated by cyber criminals who are intent on targeting our Nation's retailers and financial payment systems.

The increasing level of collaboration among cyber-criminals allows them to compartmentalize their operations, greatly increasing the sophistication of their criminal endeavors and allowing for development of expert specialization. These specialties raise both the complexity of investigating these cases, as well as the level of potential harm to companies and individuals. For example, illicit underground cybercrime market places allow criminals to buy, sell and trade malicious software, access to sensitive networks, spamming services, credit, debit and ATM card data, PII, bank account information, brokerage account information, hacking services, and counterfeit identity documents. These illicit digital marketplaces vary in size, with some of the more popular sites boasting membership of approximately 80,000 users. These digital marketplaces often use various digital currencies, and cyber criminals have made extensive use of digital currencies to pay for criminal goods and services or launder illicit proceeds.

The Secret Service has successfully investigated many underground cybercriminal marketplaces. In one such infiltration, the Secret Service initiated and conducted a three-year investigation that led to the indictment of 11 perpetrators allegedly involved in hacking nine major U.S. retailers and the theft and sale of more than 40 million credit and debit card numbers. The investigation revealed that defendants from the United States, Estonia, China and Belarus successfully obtained credit and debit card numbers by hacking into the wireless computer networks of major retailers — including TJ Maxx, BJ's Wholesale Club, Office Max, Boston Market, Barnes & Noble, Sports Authority and Dave & Buster's. Once inside the networks, these cyber criminals installed "sniffer" programs[6] that would capture card numbers, as well as password and account information, as they moved through the retailers' credit and debit processing networks. After the data was collected, the conspirators concealed the information in encrypted computer servers that they controlled in the United States and Eastern Europe. The credit and debit card numbers were then sold through online transactions to other criminals in the United States and Eastern Europe. The stolen numbers were "cashed out" by encoding card numbers on the magnetic strips of blank cards. The defendants then used these fraudulent cards to withdraw tens of thousands of dollars at a time from ATMs. The defendants were able to conceal and launder their illegal proceeds by using anonymous Internet-based digital currencies within the United States and abroad, and by channeling funds through bank accounts in Eastern Europe.[7]

In data breaches like these the effects of the criminal acts extended well beyond the companies compromised, potentially affecting millions of individual card holders. Proactive and swift law enforcement action protects consumers by preventing and limiting the fraudulent use of payment card data, identity theft, or both. Cybercrime directly impacts the U.S. economy by requiring additional investment in implementing enhanced security measures, inflicting reputational damage on U.S. firms, and direct financial losses from fraud—all costs that are ultimately passed on to consumers.

Secret Service Strategy for Combating This Threat

The Secret Service proactively investigates cybercrime using a variety of investigative means to infiltrate these transnational cyber criminal groups. As a result of these proactive investigations, the Secret Service is often the first to learn of planned or ongoing data breaches and is quick to notify financial institutions and the victim companies with actionable information to mitigate the damage from the data breach and terminate the criminal's unauthorized access to their networks. One of the most poorly understood facts regarding data breaches is that it is rarely the victim company that first discovers the criminal's unauthorized access to their network; rather it is law enforcement, financial institutions, or other third parties that identify and notify the likely victim company of the data breach by identifying the common point of origin of the sensitive data being trafficked in cybercrime marketplaces.

A trusted relationship with the victim is essential for confirming the crime, remediating the situation, beginning a criminal investigation, and collecting evidence. The Secret Service's worldwide network of 33 Electronic Crimes Task Forces (ECTF), located within our field offices, are essential for building and maintaining these trusted relationships, along with the Secret Service's commitment to protecting victim privacy.

In order to confirm the source of data breaches and to stop the continued theft of sensitive information and the exploitation of a network, the Secret Service contacts the owner of the suspected compromised computer systems. Once the victim of a data breach confirms that unauthorized access to their networks has occurred, the Secret Service works with the local U.S. Attorney's office, or appropriate state and local officials, to begin a criminal investigation of the potential violation of 18 USC § 1030. During the course of this criminal investigation, the Secret Service identifies the malware and means of access used to acquire data from the victim's computer network. In order to enable other companies to mitigate their cyber risk based on current cybercrime methods, we quickly share information concerning the cybersecurity incident with the widest audience possible, while protecting grand jury information, the integrity of ongoing criminal investigations, and the victims' privacy. We share this cybersecurity information through:

- Our Department's National Cybersecurity & Communications Integration Center (NCCIC);
- The Information Sharing and Analysis Centers (ISAC);
- Our ECTFs;
- The publication of joint industry notices;
- Our numerous partnerships developed over the past three decades in investigating cyber crimes; and,
- Contributions to leading industry and academic reports like the Verizon Data Breach Investigations Report, the Trustwave Global Security Report, and the Carnegie Mellon CERT Insider Threat Study.

As we share cybersecurity information discovered in the course of our criminal investigation, we also continue our investigation in order to apprehend and bring to justice those involved. Due to the inherent challenges in investigating transnational crime, particularly the lack of cooperation of some countries with law enforcement investigations, occasionally it takes years to finally apprehend the top tier criminals responsible. For example, Dmitriy Smilianets and Vladimir Drinkman were arrested in June 2012, as part of a multi-year investigation Secret Service investigation, while they were traveling in the Netherlands thanks to the assistance of Dutch law enforcement. The alleged total fraud loss from their cybercrimes exceeds $105 million.

As a part of our cybercrime investigations, the Secret Service also targets individuals who operate illicit infrastructure that supports the transnational organized cyber criminal. For example, in May 2013 the Secret Service, as part of a joint investigation through the Global Illicit Financial Team, shut down the digital currency provider Liberty Reserve. Liberty Reserve is alleged to have had more than one million users worldwide and to have laundered more than $6 billion in criminal proceeds. This case is believed to be the largest money laundering case ever prosecuted in the United States and is being jointly prosecuted by the U.S. Attorney's Office for the Southern District of New York and DOJ's Asset Forfeiture and Money Laundering Section. In a coordinated action with the Department of the Treasury, Liberty Reserve was identified as a financial institution of primary money laundering concern under Section 311 of the USA PATRIOT Act, effectively cutting it off from the U.S. financial system.

Collaboration with Other Federal Agencies and International Law Enforcement

While cyber-criminals operate in a world without borders, the law enforcement community does not. The increasingly multi-national, multi-jurisdictional nature of cybercrime cases has increased the time and resources needed for successful investigation and adjudication. The partnerships developed through our ECTFs, the support provided by our Criminal Investigative Division, the liaison established by our overseas offices, and the training provided to our special agents via Electronic Crimes Special Agent Program are all instrumental to the Secret Service's successful network intrusion investigations.

One example of the Secret Service's success in these investigations is the case involving Heartland Payment Systems. As described in the August 2009 indictment, a transnational organized criminal group allegedly used various network intrusion techniques to breach security and navigate the credit card processing environment. Once inside the networks, they installed "sniffer" programs to capture card numbers, as well as password and account information. The Secret Service investigation, the largest and most complex data breach investigation ever prosecuted in the United States, revealed that data from more than 130 million credit card accounts were at risk of being compromised and exfiltrated to a command and control server operated by an international group directly related to other ongoing Secret Service investigations. During the course of the investigation, the Secret Service uncovered that this international group committed other intrusions into multiple corporate networks to steal credit and debit card data. The Secret Service relied on various investigative methods, including subpoenas, search warrants, and Mutual Legal Assistance Treaty (MLAT) requests through our foreign law enforcement partners to identify three main suspects. As a result of the investigation, these primary suspects were indicted for various computer-related crimes. The lead defendant in the indictment pled guilty and was sentenced to twenty years in federal prison. This investigation is ongoing with over 100 additional victim companies identified.

Recognizing these complexities, several federal agencies are collaborating to investigate cases and identify proactive strategies. Greater collaboration within the federal, state and local law enforcement community enhances information sharing, promotes efficiency in investigations, and facilitates efforts to de-conflict in cases of concurrent jurisdiction. For example, the Secret Service has collaborated extensively with DOJ's CCIPS, which "prevents, investigates, and prosecutes computer crimes by working with other government agencies, the private sector, academic institutions, and foreign counterparts."[8] The Secret Service's ECTFs are a natural complement to CCIPS, resulting in an excellent partnership over the years. In the last decade, nearly every major cyber investigation conducted by the Secret Service has benefited from CCIPS contributions.

The Secret Service also maintains a positive relationship with the DOJ's Federal Bureau of Investigation (FBI). The Secret Service has a permanent presence at the National Cyber Investigative Joint Task Force (NCIJTF), which coordinates, integrates, and shares information related to investigations of national security cyber threats. The Secret Service also often partners with the FBI on various criminal cyber investigations. For example, in August 2010, a joint operation involving the Secret Service, FBI, and the Security Service of Ukraine (SBU), yielded the seizure of 143 computer systems – one of the largest international seizures of digital media gathered by U.S. law enforcement – consisting of 85 terabytes of data, which was eventually transferred to law enforcement authorities in the United States. The data was seized from a criminal Internet service provider located in Odessa, Ukraine, also referred to as a "Bullet Proof Hoster." Thus far, the forensic analysis of these systems has already identified a significant amount of criminal information pertaining to numerous investigations currently underway by both agencies, including malware, criminal chat communications, and PII of U.S. citizens.

The case of Vladislav Horohorin is another example of successful cooperation between the Secret Service and its law enforcement partners around the world. Mr. Horohorin, one of the world's most notorious traffickers of stolen financial information, was arrested on August 25, 2010, pursuant to a U.S. arrest warrant issued by the Secret Service. Mr. Horohorin created the first fully-automated online store which was responsible for selling stolen credit card data. Both CCIPS and the Office of International Affairs at DOJ played critical roles in this apprehension.

Furthermore, as a result of information sharing, the FBI was able to bring additional charges against Mr. Horohorin for his involvement in a Royal Bank of Scotland network intrusion. This type of cooperation is crucial if law enforcement is to be successful in disrupting and dismantling criminal organizations involved in cybercrime.

This case demonstrates the importance of international law enforcement cooperation. Through the Secret Service's 24 international field offices the Service develops close partnerships with numerous foreign law enforcement agencies in order to combat transnational crime. Successfully investigating transnational crime depends not only on the efforts of the Department of State and the DOJ's Office of International Affairs to establish and execute MLATs, and other forms of international law enforcement cooperation, but also on the personal relationships that develop between U.S. law enforcement officers and their foreign counterparts. Both the CCIPS and the Office of International Affairs at DOJ played critical roles in this apprehension. Furthermore, as a result of information sharing, the FBI was able to bring additional charges against Mr. Horohorin for his involvement in a Royal Bank of Scotland network intrusion. This type of cooperation is crucial if law enforcement is to be successful in disrupting and dismantling criminal organizations involved in cybercrime.

Within DHS, the Secret Service benefits from a close relationship with Immigration and Customs Enforcement's Homeland Security Investigations (ICE-HSI). Since 1997, the Secret Service, ICE-HSI, and IRS-CI have jointly trained on computer investigations through the Electronic Crimes Special Agent Program (ECSAP). ICE-HSI is also a member of Secret Service ECTFs, and ICE-HSI and the Secret Service have partnered on numerous cybercrime investigations including the recent take down of the digital currency Liberty Reserve.

To further its cybersecurity information sharing efforts, the Secret Service has strengthened its relationship with the National Protection and Programs Directorate (NPPD), including the NCCIC. As the Secret Service identifies malware, suspicious IPs and other information through its criminal investigations, it shares information with our Department's NCCIC. The Secret Service continues to build upon its full-time presence at NCCIC to coordinate its cyber programs with other federal agencies.

As a part of these efforts, and to ensure that information is shared in a timely and effective manner, the Secret Service has personnel assigned to the following DHS and non-DHS entities:

- NPPD's National Cybersecurity & Communications Integration Center (NCCIC);
- NPPD's Office of Infrastructure Protection;
- DHS's Science and Technology Directorate (S&T);
- DOJ National Cyber Investigative Joint Task Force (NCIJTF);
- Each FBI Joint Terrorism Task Force (JTTF), including the National JTTF;
- Department of the Treasury - Office of Terrorist Financing and Financial Crimes (TFFC);
- Department of the Treasury - Financial Crimes Enforcement Network (FinCEN);
- Central Intelligence Agency;
- DOJ, International Organized Crime and Intelligence Operations Center (IOC-2);
- Drug Enforcement Administration's Special Operations Division;
- EUROPOL; and
- INTERPOL.

The Secret Service is committed to ensuring that all its information sharing activities comply with applicable laws, regulations, and policies, including those that pertain to privacy and civil liberties.

SECRET SERVICE FRAMEWORK

To protect our financial infrastructure, industry, and the American public, the Secret Service has adopted a multi-faceted approach to aggressively combat cyber and computer-related crimes.

Electronic Crimes Task Forces

In 1995, the Secret Service New York Field Office established the New York Electronic Crimes Task Force (ECTF) to combine the resources of academia, the private sector, and local, state and federal law enforcement agencies to combat computer-based threats to our financial payment systems and critical infrastructures. In 2001, Congress directed the Secret Service to establish a nationwide network of ECTFs to "prevent, detect, and investigate various forms of electronic crimes, including potential terrorist attacks against critical infrastructure and financial payment systems."[9]

Secret Service field offices currently operate 33 ECTFs, including two based overseas in Rome, Italy, and London, England. Membership in our ECTFs includes: over 4,000 private sector partners; over 2,500 international, federal, state and local law enforcement partners; and over 350 academic partners. By joining our ECTFs, our partners benefit from the resources, information, expertise and advanced research provided by our international network of members while focusing on issues with significant regional impact.

Cyber Intelligence Section

Another example of our partnership approach with private industry is our Cyber Intelligence Section (CIS) which analyzes evidence collected as a part of Secret Service investigations and disseminates information in support of Secret Service investigations worldwide and generates new investigative leads based upon its findings. CIS leverages technology and information obtained through private sector partnerships to monitor developing technologies and trends in the financial payments industry for information that may be used to enhance the Secret Service's capabilities to prevent and mitigate attacks against the financial and critical infrastructures. CIS also has an operational unit that investigates international cyber-criminals involved in cyberintrusions, identity theft, credit card fraud, bank fraud, and other computer-related crimes. The information and coordination provided by CIS is a crucial element to successfully investigating, prosecuting, and dismantling international criminal organizations.

Electronic Crimes Special Agent Program

A central component of the Secret Service's cyber-crime investigations is its Electronic Crimes Special Agent Program (ECSAP), which is comprised of nearly 1,400 Secret Service special agents who have received at least one of three levels of computer crimes-related training.

Level I – Basic Investigation of Computers and Electronic Crimes (BICEP): The BICEP training program focuses on the investigation of electronic crimes and provides a brief overview of several aspects involved with electronic crimes investigations. This program provides Secret Service agents and our state and local law enforcement partners with a basic understanding of computers and electronic crime investigations and is now part of our core curriculum for newly hired special agents.

Level II – Network Intrusion Responder (ECSAP-NI): ECSAP-NI training provides special agents with specialized training and equipment that allows them to respond to and investigate network intrusions. These may include intrusions into financial sector computer systems, corporate storage servers, or various other targeted platforms. The Level II trained agent will be able to identify critical artifacts that will allow for effective investigation of identity theft, malicious hacking, unauthorized access, and various other related electronic crimes.

Level III – Computer Forensics (ECSAP-CF): ECSAP-CF training provides special agents with specialized training and equipment that allows them to investigate and forensically obtain digital evidence to be utilized in the prosecution of various electronic crimes cases, as well as criminally-focused protective intelligence cases.

These agents are deployed in Secret Service field offices throughout the world and have received extensive training in forensic identification, as well as the preservation and retrieval of electronically stored evidence. ECSAP-trained agents are computer investigative specialists, qualified to conduct examinations on all types of electronic evidence. These special agents are equipped to investigate the continually evolving arena of electronic crimes and have proven invaluable in the successful prosecution of criminal groups involved in computer fraud, bank fraud, identity theft, access device fraud and various other electronic crimes targeting our financial institutions and private sector.

National Computer Forensics Institute

The National Computer Forensics Institute (NCFI) initiative is the result of a partnership between the Secret Service, NPPD, the State of Alabama, and the Alabama District Attorney's Association. The goal of this facility is to provide a national standard of training for a variety of electronic crimes investigations. The program offers state and local law enforcement officers, prosecutors, and judges the training necessary to conduct computer forensics examinations. Investigators are trained to respond to network intrusion incidents and to conduct electronic crimes investigations. Since opening in 2008, the institute has held over 110 cyber and digital forensics courses in 13 separate subjects and trained and equipped more than 2,500 state and local officials, including more than 1,600 police investigators, 570 prosecutors and 180 judges from all 50 states and three U.S. territories. These NCFI graduates represent more than 1,000 agencies nationwide.

Partnerships with Academia

In August 2000, the Secret Service and Carnegie Mellon University Software Engineering Institute (SEI) established the Secret Service CERT[10] Liaison Program to provide technical support, opportunities for research and development, as well as public outreach and education to more than 150 scientists and researchers in the fields of computer and network security, malware analysis, forensic development, training and education. Supplementing this effort is research into emerging technologies being used by cyber-criminals and development of technologies and techniques to combat them.

The primary goals of the program are: to broaden the Secret Service's knowledge of software engineering and networked systems security; to expand and strengthen partnerships and relationships with the technical and academic communities; partner with CERT-SEI and Carnegie Mellon University to support research and development to improve the security of cyberspace and improve the ability of law enforcement to investigate crimes in a digital age; and to present the results of this partnership at the quarterly meetings of our ECTFs.

In August 2004, the Secret Service partnered with CERT-SEI to publish the first "Insider Threat Study" examining the illicit cyber activity and insider fraud in the banking and finance sector. Due to the overwhelming response to this initial study, the Secret Service and CERT-SEI, in partnership with DHS Science & Technology (S&T), updated the study and released the most recent version just last year, which is published at http://www.cert.org/insider_threat/.

To improve law enforcement's ability to investigate crimes involving mobile devices, the Secret Service opened the Cell Phone Forensic Facility at the University of Tulsa in 2008. This facility has a three-pronged mission: (1) training federal, state and local law enforcement agents in embedded device forensics; (2) developing novel hardware and software solutions for extracting and analyzing digital evidence from embedded devices; and (3) applying the hardware and software solutions to support criminal investigations conducted by the Secret Service and its partner agencies. To date, investigators trained at the Cell Phone Forensic Facility have completed more than 6,500 examinations on cell phone and embedded devices nationwide. Secret Service agents assigned to the Tulsa facility have contributed to over 300 complex cases that have required the development of sophisticated techniques and tools to extract critical evidence.

These collaborations with academia, among others, have produced valuable innovations that have helped strengthen the cyber ecosystem and improved law enforcement's ability to investigate cybercrime. The Secret Service will continue to partner closely with academia and DHS S&T, particularly the Cyber Forensics Working Group, to support research and development of innovate tools and methods to support criminal investigations.

LEGISLATIVE ACTION TO COMBAT DATA BREACHES

While there is no single solution to prevent data breaches of U.S. customer information, legislative action could help to improve the Nation's cybersecurity, reduce regulatory costs on U.S. companies, and strengthen law enforcement's ability to conduct effective investigations. The Administration previously proposed law enforcement provisions related to computer security through a letter from OMB Director Lew to Congress on May 12, 2011, highlighting the importance of additional tools to combat emerging criminal practices. We continue to support changes like these that will keep up with rapidly-evolving technologies and uses.

CONCLUSION

The Secret Service is committed to safeguarding the Nation's financial payment systems by investigating and dismantling criminal organizations involved in cybercrime. Responding to the growth in these types of crimes and the level of sophistication these criminals employ requires significant resources and greater collaboration among law enforcement and its public and private sector partners. Accordingly, the Secret Service dedicates significant resources to improving investigative techniques, providing training for law enforcement partners, and raising public awareness. The Secret Service will continue to be innovative in its approach to cybercrime and cyber security and is pleased that the Committee recognizes the magnitude of these issues and the evolving nature of these crimes.

End Notes

[1] Beginning in 1970, and over the course of three years, the chief teller at the Park Avenue branch of New York's Union Dime Savings Bank manipulated the account information on the bank's computer system to embezzle over $1.5 million from hundreds of customer accounts. This early example of cyber crime not only illustrates the long history of cyber crime, but the difficulty companies have in identifying and stopping cyber criminals in a timely manner—a trend that continues today.

[2] *See* 18 USC § 1030

[3] *See* 18 USC § 1029

[4] *See* 18 USC § 1029(e)(1)

[5] *See* 18 USC § 1029(d) & 1030(d)(1)

[6] Sniffers are programs that detect particular information transiting computer networks, and can be used by criminals to acquire sensitive information from computer systems.

[7] Additional information on the criminal use of digital currencies can be referenced in testimony provided by U.S. Secret Service Special Agent in Charge Edward Lowery before the Senate Homeland Security and Governmental Affairs Committee in a hearing titled, "Beyond Silk Road: Potential Risks, Threats, and Promises of Virtual Currencies" (November 18, 2013).

[8] U.S. Department of Justice. (n.d.). *Computer Crime & Intellectual Property Section: About CCIPS.* Retrieved from http://www.justice.gov/criminal/cybercrime/ccips.html

[9] *See* Public Law 107-56 Section 105 (appears as note following 18 U.S.C. § 3056).

[10] CERT—not an acronym—conducts empirical research and analysis to develop and transition socio-technical solutions to combat insider cyber threats.

In: The Target Store Data Breaches
Editor: Marianna Hardy
ISBN: 978-1-63321-269-5

Chapter 10

STATEMENT OF MYTHILI RAMAN, ACTING ASSISTANT ATTORNEY GENERAL, CRIMINAL DIVISION, UNITED STATES DEPARTMENT OF JUSTICE. HEARING ON "PRIVACY IN THE DIGITAL AGE: PREVENTING DATA BREACHES AND COMBATING CYBERCRIME"*

Good afternoon, Chairman Leahy, Ranking Member Grassley, and Members of the Committee. Thank you for the opportunity to appear before the Committee today to discuss the Department of Justice's fight against cybercrime. I also particularly want to thank the Chair for holding this hearing and for his continued leadership on these important issues.

At the Department of Justice, we are devoting significant resources and energy to fighting computer hacking and other types of cybercrime. The recent revelations about the massive thefts of financial information from large retail stores have served as a stark reminder to all of us about how vulnerable we are to cyber criminals who are determined to steal our personal information. The Justice Department is more committed than ever to ensuring that the full range of government enforcement tools is brought to bear in the fight against cybercrime.

* This is an edited, reformatted and augmented version of a statement presented February 4, 2014 before a hearing of the Senate Judiciary Committee.

Cybercrime has increased dramatically over the last decade, and our financial infrastructure has suffered repeated cyber intrusions. As we all know, it is becoming far too commonplace an occurrence that our email accounts are hijacked, our financial information siphoned away, and our personal information compromised. The technology revolution – which has brought enormous benefits to individuals, U.S. companies and our economy as a whole – has also facilitated these criminal activities, making available a wide array of new methods that identity thieves can use to access and exploit the personal information of others. Skilled criminal hackers are now able to perpetrate large-scale data breaches that leave, in some cases, tens of millions of individuals at risk of identity theft. Today's criminals, who often sit on the other side of the world, can hack into computer systems of universities, merchants, financial institutions, credit card processing companies, and data processors to steal large volumes of sensitive and valuable information. They then peddle the stolen information to other criminals, use the information for their own financial gain, or sometimes even terrorize and extort their victims.

Last December, Target, the second-largest U.S. discount chain, announced that credit and debit card data for as many as 40 million consumers who shopped in its stores between November 27 and December 15 may have been compromised. Target then disclosed on January 10 that thieves had also accessed the personal information, including names, phone numbers, home addresses, and/or email addresses, of as many as 70 million people – information that is valued by criminals because it can be used to lure victims with fake emails or hack into other accounts. The U.S. Secret Service, within the Department of Homeland Security, and the Department of Justice are investigating this massive data breach.

A few days later, retailer Neiman Marcus Inc. reported that it also was the victim of a suspected cyberattack over the holidays in which some of its customers' credit card information may have been stolen. Target and Neiman Marcus are just two of the latest known victims.

The Justice Department is vigorously responding to hacking and other cybercrimes through the tenacious work of the Criminal Division's Computer Crime and Intellectual Property Section, also known as CCIPS, which partners with Computer Hacking and Intellectual Property Coordinators in U.S. Attorney's Offices across the country as part of a network of almost 300 Justice Department cybercrime prosecutors. In addition, the Federal Bureau of Investigation has made combating cyber threats one of its top national priorities, working through Cyber Task Forces in each of its 56 field offices and continuing to strengthen the National Cyber Investigative Joint Task

Force. Every day, these prosecutors and agents strive to hold to account cyber criminals who victimize Americans.

Consider, for instance, the case of Vladislav Horohorin, which was prosecuted here in the District of Columbia by CCIPS and the United States Attorney's Office, based on an investigation by the FBI and U.S. Secret Service. Horohorin, known by the online nickname "BadB," used online criminal forums to sell stolen credit and debit card information to individuals around the world to enable fraudulent transactions by other cyber criminals. At the time of his arrest, he possessed more than 2.5 million stolen credit and debit card numbers. In one instance, he participated in a criminal group that, in a single 12-hour crime spree, stole over $9.4 million through fraudulent transactions at over 2,100 ATMs in 280 cities around the world. As a result of a massive investigation spanning several years – and several countries – we located and charged him, and he was arrested after leaving Russia for France. In April 2013, Horohorin was sentenced to serve 88 months in prison.

Our investigation of the Coreflood botnet is another example of our commitment to stopping massive computer crimes by using the most innovative law enforcement techniques. A botnet is a network of secretly hacked computers, sometimes numbering in the millions, which are located in homes, schools, and offices. The computers are infected with sophisticated malicious software, or "malware," and once the malware is installed, hackers can put these bots to countless illegal uses. The Coreflood botnet, for example, hijacked hundreds of thousands of computers for the purpose of stealing private personal and financial information – including usernames and passwords – from unsuspecting computer users. In one example, the Coreflood botnet software illegally monitored Internet communications between a computer user and her bank, took over an online banking session, and then emptied the user's bank account. Overall losses from the scheme were staggering, estimated to be in the tens of millions of dollars.

Although the individuals controlling the Coreflood network resided overseas and were largely outside the direct reach of U.S. law enforcement, in 2011, CCIPS, the United States Attorney's Office for the District of Connecticut, and the FBI used a combination of civil and criminal legal authorities to seize key control servers, shut down the network, and work with private sector partners to help disinfect victims' computer systems. Among other things, as part of this ground-breaking law enforcement operation, the Justice Department obtained a court order authorizing the government to respond to signals sent from infected computers in the United States to stop the Coreflood software from running, and thus to prevent further harm to hundreds of thousands of Americans whose computers were under the control of the botnet. And, in a relatively short period of time, the Coreflood botnet was dismantled.

The Department has continued to place a high priority on arresting and deterring those who create botnets. CCIPS and the U.S. Attorney's Office in Atlanta just last week announced the guilty plea of a Russian citizen named Aleksandr Panin for developing and distributing malware called "SpyEye." The SpyEye malware created botnets that stole personal and financial information such as credit card information, banking credentials, usernames, passwords, and personal identification numbers. Panin sold his software to at least 154 criminal "clients," who in turn used it to infect an estimated 1.4 million computers around the world. The FBI arrested Panin on July 1, 2013, while he was flying through Hartsfield-Jackson Atlanta International Airport.

Hacking can have terrifying consequences even when conducted on a smaller scale, and we have vigorously pursued hackers who have used the Internet to invade Americans' privacy. In 2011, for example, in a case investigated by the FBI, the United States Attorney's Office in Los Angeles successfully prosecuted a hacker named Luis Mijangos. Mijangos hacked for sexual thrill. He infected the computers of victims with malicious software that gave him complete control over their computers. He deliberately targeted teens and young women, reading their emails, turning on their computer microphones and listening to conversations taking place in their homes, and, most importantly for him, watching them through their webcams as they undressed. Even more frightening, Mijangos then extorted certain victims by threatening to post intimate pictures on the Internet unless the victims provided him with even more salacious images or videos of themselves. When one victim shared Mijangos's threats with a friend, Mijangos retaliated by posting nude pictures of the victim on her friend's social networking page. In another instance, Mijangos had infected the computers of a college student, her boyfriend, and her roommate. When the victim called her boyfriend, and they discussed calling the police, Mijangos reportedly sent the boyfriend an anonymous instant message that said: "I know you're talking to each other right now!" The victim then decided to call the police. But when she did, she got a message, too. "I know you just called the police," he wrote. His message was unmistakable: he was in control; he knew everything; and he had the power to hurt the victim further if she reported the crime. At the time of his arrest, FBI computer forensics experts had determined that Mijangos had infected more than 100 computers that were used by approximately 230 individuals, at least 44 of them minors. The Court sentenced Mijangos to 72 months in federal prison.

There are many other examples of the Department's recent work to bring cyber criminals to justice. There is the takedown of Silk Road, a hidden website designed to enable its users to buy and sell illegal drugs and other unlawful goods and services, and charges against the alleged operator of the site by the U.S. Attorney's Offices for the Southern District of New York and the District of Maryland. There is the prosecution by CCIPS and the U.S. Attorney's Office in New Hampshire of Adrian-Tiberiu Oprea, a Romanian who recently received a 15-year sentence in September for leading an international, multimillion-dollar scheme to remotely hack into and steal unsuspecting customers' payment card data from U.S. merchants' computers. The case was investigated by the U.S. Secret Service. There is the recent indictment by CCIPS and the U.S. Attorney's Office for the Western District of Wisconsin of Sinovel Wind Group Co. Ltd., a China-based manufacturer and exporter of wind turbines, which is alleged to have stolen trade secrets from an American company for the purpose of producing wind turbines and retrofitting existing wind turbines with the stolen technology. And on January 23, the FBI arrested two men for conspiring to hack into victims' email accounts to steal nude photos that were later posted on the "revenge porn" website isanyoneup.com. The U.S. Attorney's Office for the Central District of California charged the men with violating the Computer Fraud and Abuse Act.

The recent disclosures about the massive data breaches at retailers have underscored that cybercrime is a real, present threat, and one that is growing. Cyber criminals steal the personal and financial information of individuals, carry out Distributed Denial of Service (or DDOS)[1] attacks on networks, and purloin sensitive corporate or military data. These criminals can easily prey on victims halfway around the world. They sometimes use virtual currencies to enrich themselves while hiding their identities and avoiding leaving their fingerprints in the traditional banking system. Despite these challenges, the Justice Department is staying ahead of these threats. We are using all of the tools available to us to identify cyber criminals, wherever in the world they are located, break up their networks, and bring them to justice. We are developing meaningful partnerships with foreign law enforcement to strengthen our collective capacity to fight cybercrime. And we use our tools responsibly and consistent with established legal safeguards that protect against abuse. But without the tools we have been provided, we would not be able to bring offenders to justice. And we must ensure that the statutes we enforce keep up with technology so that we can keep pace with the cyber criminals, who are constantly developing new tactics and methods.

COMPUTER FRAUD AND ABUSE ACT

In addition to the important law enforcement techniques that we must use to successfully investigate cyber criminals, our prosecutors also rely on substantive criminal statutes to bring cyber criminals to justice. One of the most important of these laws is the Computer Fraud and Abuse Act, also called the "CFAA." The CFAA is the primary Federal law against hacking. It protects the public against criminals who hack into computers to steal information, install malicious software, and delete files. The CFAA, in short, reflects our baseline expectation that people are entitled to have control over their own computers and are entitled to trust that information they store in their computers remains safe.

The CFAA was first enacted in 1986, at a time when the problem of cybercrime was still in its infancy. Over the years, a series of measured, modest changes have been made to the CFAA to reflect new technologies and means of committing crimes and to equip law enforcement with tools to respond to changing threats. The CFAA has not been amended since 2008, and the intervening years have again created the need for the enactment of modest, incremental changes. The Administration's May 2011 legislative proposal proposed revisions to keep Federal criminal law up-to-date. We continue to support changes like these that will keep up with rapidly-evolving technologies and uses.

DETERRING INSIDER THREATS

Another portion of the CFAA that has received considerable attention is the way that the law addresses the threat posed by insiders – those who have some right to access a system but who abuse that right, such as employees of a business who unlawfully make off with their employers' intellectual property. The CFAA addresses this problem by criminalizing conduct by those who "exceed authorized access" to a protected computer.

Some commentators have contended that the CFAA's provision criminalizing exceeding authorized access should be limited or abolished because the provision is subject to misuse or overuse. Some have worried, for example, that the statute permits prosecution of people who merely lie about their age when going to a dating site, or harmlessly violate the terms of service of an email provider. To that end, we are open to addressing these concerns by working with Congress to develop appropriate statutory amendments, such as new statutory thresholds regarding the value or sensitivity of the information improperly accessed under 1030(a)(2), or new language making more explicit that the statute does not permit prosecution based on access restrictions that are not clearly understood.

At the same time, insider hackers pose a serious threat to American businesses and citizens. Examples of insiders include employees at a credit card company or stock broker who regularly deal with sensitive information. There is generally no way to encrypt and password-protect every piece of data on a system to eliminate the insider threat, because employees need to be able access the data to do their jobs. Thus, written policies between employers and employees – which are simply a contractual means of ensuring trust – are an important way to secure information. Violating these written restrictions harms businesses. Just as businesses justifiably rely on the criminal law to deter thefts of physical property, so they also should be able to rely on it to deter misappropriation of their private, sensitive data – data that is often far more valuable than equipment or supplies.

In recent years, two courts of appeals have interpreted the CFAA to bar certain "insider" cases, creating a circuit split. Compare *United States v. Nosal*, 676 F.3d 854 (9th Cir. 2012) (*en banc*) and *WEC Carolina Energy Solutions LLC v. Miller*, 687 F.3d 199 (4th Cir. 2012), with *United States v. John*, 597 F.3d 263 (5th Cir. 2010); *United States v. Rodriguez*, 628 F.3d 1258 (11th Cir. 2010); and *Int'l Airport Ctrs., LLC v. Citrin*, 440 F.3d 418 (7th Cir. 2006). Specifically, the Fourth and Ninth Circuits have interpreted the statute not to permit prosecution as long as an insider was authorized to access the database or information in question for any purpose. Under this interpretation, the CFAA would not apply where a police officer accessed an arrest record for the purpose of harassing a romantic rival, because the officer was authorized to access the records to assist in criminal investigations. Similarly, under this interpretation, the CFAA would not apply where a bank employee accessed customer records for the purpose of selling them to organized crime members, because the employee was authorized to access the records to resolve customer complaints. This interpretation makes it substantially more challenging for DOJ to protect American companies from the misappropriation of their intellectual property and sensitive data – misappropriation that may also directly harm American citizens when that data includes their personal or financial information.

We look forward to working with Congress to address these important issues.

DATA BREACH NOTIFICATION

While the Justice Department continues to use all of the tools at its disposal to combat cybercrime, the Administration recommends the establishment of a strong, uniform Federal standard requiring certain types of businesses to report data breaches and thefts of electronic personally identifiable information. Businesses should be required to provide prompt notice to consumers in the wake of a breach. We should balance the need to safeguard consumers and hold compromised entities accountable, while setting clear standards that avoid undue burdens on industry. We should include a safe harbor for breaches with no reasonable risk of harm or fraud. This approach would protect the privacy of individuals while holding firms accountable for failure to safeguard personal data.

In 2011, the Administration put forth a package of recommended cybersecurity amendments that included a data breach notification proposal.[2] The 2011 proposal is based upon the belief that American consumers should know when they are at risk of identity theft or other harms because of a data security breach. In addition, to strengthen the tools available to law enforcement to investigate data security breaches and to combat identity theft, the proposal would require that business entities notify the Federal government of a data security breach in a timely fashion so that law enforcement can promptly pursue the perpetrators of cyber intrusions and identity theft. The proposal has several sections of particular note.

First, under this proposal, following the discovery of a security breach, business entities must notify any individual whose sensitive, personally identifiable information has been, or is reasonably believed to have been, accessed or acquired, unless there is no reasonable risk of harm. Business entities covered under this requirement are those that use, access, transmit, store, dispose of, or collect sensitive, personally identifiable information about more than 10,000 people during any 12-month period. But the Administration believes that business entities which have demonstrated that they have effective data breach prevention programs should be exempt from notice to individuals if a risk assessment concludes that there is no reasonable risk that a security breach has harmed, or will harm, the individuals whose information was compromised.

The proposal would also recognize that such harm may be avoided where the stolen data has been rendered unusable by criminals; for example, through encryption, or through programs that block unauthorized financial transactions and provide effective notice to affected victims. The proposal also includes certain exceptions for notice that would impair law enforcement investigations or national security.

Because of the importance of bringing the perpetrators of data breaches to justice, the Administration's proposal would also require business entities to notify law enforcement agencies if the security breach involves (1) the sensitive information of more than 5,000 people; (2) a database or other data system containing sensitive information of more than 500,000 people nationwide; (3) databases owned by the Federal government; or (4) primarily the sensitive information of Federal employees and contractors involved in national security or law enforcement. Businesses would report to a single entity that would then promptly disseminate the reported information to key Federal law enforcement agencies. In recognition of the time-sensitivity of data breach investigations, the notice required under this section would be provided as promptly as possible, but no later than 72 hours before notification to an individual or 10 days after discovery of the events requiring notice, whichever comes first.

Millions of Americans every year are faced with the potential for fraud and identity theft from online breaches of their sensitive, personally identifiable information. The nation clearly needs strong protections for consumers' rights and privacy, and accountability for businesses that do not safeguard credit card and social security numbers, names and addresses, medical records, and other sensitive information. The Administration's proposal creates a strong national standard to notify consumers with clear, actionable information when their personal information is compromised. Responsible entities will be held accountable through these disclosures. At the same time, a consistent national standard and reasonable exemptions for harmless breaches will reduce unnecessary compliance costs. This proposal meets the dual challenge of ensuring privacy, security, and safety without burdening economic prosperity and innovation.

ACCESS DEVICE FRAUD

To ensure that we can take action when cyber criminals acting overseas steal data from U.S. financial institutions, we also recommend a modification to what is known as the access device fraud statute, 18 U.S.C. § 1029. One of the most common motivations for hacking crime is to obtain financial information. The access device fraud statute proscribes the unlawful possession and use of "access devices," such as credit card numbers and devices such as credit card embossing machines. Not only do lone individuals commit this crime, but, more and more, organized criminal enterprises have formed to commit such intrusions and to exploit the stolen data through fraud.

The Department of Justice recommends that the statute be expanded to prosecute offenders in foreign countries who directly and significantly harm United States financial institutions and citizens. Currently, a criminal who trades in credit card information issued by a U.S. financial institution, but who otherwise does not take one of certain enumerated actions within the jurisdiction of the United States, cannot be prosecuted under section 1029(a)(3). Such scenarios are not merely hypothetical. United States law enforcement agencies have identified foreign-based individuals selling vast quantities of credit card numbers issued by U.S. financial institutions where there is no evidence that those criminals took a specific step within the United States to traffic in the data. The United States has a compelling interest in prosecuting such individuals given the harm to U.S. financial institutions and American citizens, and the statute should be revised to cover this sort of criminal conduct.

DETERRING THE SPREAD OF CELL PHONE SPYING

The Department of Justice further recommends a legislative change to enable law enforcement to seize the profits of those who use cell phone spyware. The spread of computers and cellular phones in recent years has created a new market in malicious software that allows perpetrators to intercept victims' communications without their knowledge or consent. This is illegal under current law, and current law also provides that law enforcement can forfeit the surreptitious interception devices themselves. It does not, however, enable forfeiture of the proceeds of the sale or use of those devices, or the forfeiture of any property used to facilitate their manufacture, advertising, or distribution. Further, the surreptitious interception of communications is currently not listed as a predicate offense in the money laundering statute, 18 U.S.C. § 1956. Because perpetrators of these crimes often act from abroad, making it more difficult to prosecute them, it is particularly important that law enforcement be able to seize the money that the criminals make from engaging in this criminal surveillance, and seize the equipment they use.

SELLING ACCESS TO BOTNETS

We also recommend amending current law to address the proliferation of botnets, such as the Coreflood botnet I discussed earlier. Botnets can be used for various nefarious purposes, including theft of personal or financial information, the dissemination of spam, and cyberattacks, such as Distributed Denial of Service attacks. But creators and operators of botnets do not always commit those crimes themselves – frequently they sell, or even rent, access to the infected computers to others. The CFAA does not clearly cover such trafficking in botnets, even though trafficking in infected computers is clearly illegitimate, and can be essential to furthering other criminal activity. We thus propose that the CFAA be amended to cover trafficking in access to botnets.

In addition, section 1030(a)(6) presently requires proof of intent to defraud. Such intent is often difficult to prove because the traffickers of unauthorized access to computers often have a wrongful purpose other than the commission of fraud, or do not know or care why their customers are seeking unauthorized access to other people's computers. This has made it more challenging in many cases for prosecutors to identify a provable offense even when they can establish beyond a reasonable doubt that individuals are selling access to thousands of infected computers. We therefore recommend that Congress consider amending the CFAA to address this shortcoming.

CONCLUSION

I very much appreciate the opportunity to discuss with you the ways in which the Department protects American citizens and businesses by aggressively investigating and prosecuting hackers – both outsiders and insiders. We understand how devastating it is to victims of cybercrime who have their personal and financial information siphoned away, whether by hackers on the other side of the world or by insiders at a company that might hold their personal information. The Justice Department is committed to using the full range of investigative tools and laws available to us to fight these crimes and protect Americans. And, we will continue to use these tools responsibly.

Thank you for the opportunity to discuss the Department's work in this area, and I look forward to answering any questions you might have.

End Notes

[1] A Distributed Denial of Service attack is one in which a criminal uses many compromised computer systems to send information to a single target computer. The flood of incoming information to the target computer makes it unable to function correctly, thereby denying service to the legitimate users of the system.

[2] The Administration's Privacy and Innovation Blueprint, released in February 2012, also called for a data breach notification law.

In: The Target Store Data Breaches
Editor: Marianna Hardy
ISBN: 978-1-63321-269-5

Chapter 11

WRITTEN QUESTIONS FOR THE RECORD OF CHAIRMAN LEAHY FOR JOHN J. MULLIGAN, EXECUTIVE VICE PRESIDENT AND CHIEF FINANCIAL OFFICER, TARGET CORPORATION*

1. At the February 4, 2014 hearing, you testified that Target suffered two data breaches: The first affected the payment information of approximately 40 million customers. A second data breach affected the sensitive personal information of approximately 70 million customers.

a. Did both of these data breaches involve the same malware and the same perpetrator(s)? Please explain.

Chairman Leahy, I appreciate the opportunity to clarify the details surrounding the breach and the impacted data. We have consistently stated that the breach affected two types of data: payment card data which affected approximately 40 million guests and partial personal data which affected up to 70 million guests. The theft of the payment card data affected guests who shopped at our U.S. stores from November 27 through December 18. The theft of partial personal data included name, mailing address, phone number or email address.

* This is an edited, reformatted and augmented version of written questions and answers presented February 11, 2014 to Senator Patrick Leahy, Chairman of the Senate Judiciary Committee.

We now know that the intruder stole a vendor's credentials to access our system and place malware on our point-of-sale registers. The malware was designed to capture payment card data from the magnetic strip of credit and debit cards prior to encryption within our system. The intruder also accessed partial personal data for up to 70 million guests. This partial personal data included name, address, email address and telephone number.

While the investigation is still active and ongoing, we believe the same attacker is responsible for the theft of both sets of data.

> b. Vast amounts of stored consumer data can become an attractive target for cyber thieves. Does Target store its customers' personally identifiable information on its computer systems? If so, what steps does Target take to protect this sensitive data from data breaches or other cyber attacks?

Target stores its guests' data on its computer systems. For many years, Target has invested significant capital and resources in security technology, personnel and processes, including firewalls, malware detection software, intrusion detection and prevention capabilities and data loss prevention tools. We perform internal and external validation and benchmarking assessments. Target's last assessment for compliance with the Payment Card Industry Data Security Standards ("PCI DSS") was completed on September 20, 2013 by Trustwave. On that date, Trustwave certified Target as compliant with PCI DSS.

> c. Does Target notify its customers about the company's policy on the collection and retention of customer data?

At Target, we want our guests to know how we collect, use, share, and protect information about them. By interacting with Target, our guests consent to use of information that is collected or submitted as described in our privacy policy (link to our privacy policy included below).
http://www.target.com/spot/privacy-policy#?lnk=fnavtspc22&intc=28074|null

> d. Do Target customers have the ability to opt out of any program involving the collection or retention of their personal information?

We provide our guests with choices about receiving marketing from Target and sharing of personal information with other companies for their marketing purposes. Our privacy policy provides our guests with information related to the collection, use, sharing and protection of information about them.
http://www.target.com/spot/privacy-policy#?lnk=fnavtspc22&intc=28074|null

2. During the hearing, you discussed your support for so-called "Chip and Pin" technology for point of sale transactions.

a. When do you anticipate that Target will adopt Chip and Pin technology at its stores?

At Target, we've been working for years towards adoption of this technology. Since the breach, we are accelerating our own $100 million investment to put chip-enabled technology in place. Our goal is to implement this technology in our stores and on our proprietary REDcards by early 2015, more than six months ahead of our previous plan.

b. Do you have any concerns about this technology?

For consumers, this technology differs in important ways from what is widely used in the United States today. The standard credit and debit cards we use now have a magnetic stripe containing account information. When first introduced, that stripe was an innovation. But in today's world, more is needed. The latest "smart cards" have tiny microprocessor chips that encrypt the personal data shared with the sales terminals used by merchants. This change is important because even if a thief manages to steal a smart card number, it's useless without the chip.

In addition, requiring the use of a four-digit personal identification number (PIN) to complete a sales transaction would provide even greater safety. While there is no consensus across the business community on the use of PINs in conjunction with chip-enabled cards, Target supports the goal and will work toward adoption of the practice in our own stores and more widely.

In the United Kingdom, where smart card technology is widely used, financial losses associated with lost or stolen cards are at their lowest levels since 1999 and have fallen by 67 percent since 2004, according to industry estimates. In Canada, where Target and others have adopted smart cards, losses from card skimming were reduced by 72 percent from 2008 to 2012, according to industry estimates.

> c. Has Target explored any other payment processing methods to help protect the privacy of sensitive financial and consumer data during the payment process?

Target is investing in solutions that will make mobile transactions more secure. We know work is needed to strengthen protections for e-commerce, an important long-term goal. In the meantime, adopting chip-enabled cards would be a clear step in the right direction.

3. Has the investigation into the data breach at Target prompted any changes in Target's security of online transactions or stored customer data? If so, please explain.

In addition to the active and ongoing criminal investigation, we are in the midst of a comprehensive, end-to-end review of our entire network. It is our expectation that the findings from the internal review will provide us with opportunities to make security enhancements as appropriate.

INDEX

A

B

C

D

E

F

G

H

I

J

K

L

M

N

O

P

T

U

V

W

Y